Pastoral Care in the
Small Membership Church

Pastoral Care
in the Small Membership Church

JAMES L. KILLEN, JR.

Abingdon Press
Nashville

PASTORAL CARE IN THE SMALL MEMBERSHIP CHURCH

Copyright © 2005 by Abingdon Press

All rights reserved.

This book is printed on acid-free paper.

Library of Congress Cataloging-in-Publication Data

Killen, James L.
Pastoral care in the small membership church / James L. Killen, Jr.
   p. cm.
ISBN 0-687-34326-7   (binding: pbk. : alk. paper)
1.Small churches.   2. Pastoral care.   I. Title

BV637.8.K55   2005
253—dc22   2004020211

Scripture quotations are from the *New Revised Standard Version of the Bible,* copyright 1989, Division of Christian Education of the National Council of the Churches of Christ in the United States of America. Used by permission. All rights reserved.

05 06 07 08 09 10 11 12 13 14—10 9 8 7 6 5 4 3 2 1

MANUFACTURED IN THE UNITED STATES OF AMERICA

Contents

114376

Preface

I remember the day when the adventure began. One week after my ordination and two weeks before my wedding, I left the city that had been my home and drove north for most of a day. In late afternoon, I stopped in front of the little white church surrounded by big oak trees that would be the meeting place of the first congregation of which I was to be pastor, and the little white house built of salvaged lumber that would be my new home. I stepped out of the car into warm, pine-scented stillness. I could hear nothing but the sound of a gentle breeze and the call of a bobwhite. I looked around and realized that I was in a place that was very different and very beautiful.

Within minutes, an old pickup truck rattled to a stop in front of the house. A suntanned man in denim work clothes and a straw hat got out and rambled toward me with a bashful smile on his face. He explained that he was the chairman of the Administrative Board and my nearest neighbor. He had been watching for me. He showed me around, invited me to come to his house for supper, and told me that choir practice would be at "dark thirty." I was on my way to learning to be a pastor.

This book is intended to be an introduction to pastoral care for pastors of small membership churches. The primary resource for the writing has been my experience. I have served as a pastor for forty-five years. About half of that was in small membership churches with average attendance of fewer than one hundred. I have made many mistakes and learned from them. I have had the advantage of a great deal of reading and many training events that helped equip me for that ministry. I have also had the advantage of insights from the experiences that other pastors have shared with me.

I realize that I am writing for a very diverse group. A few years ago, I had the privilege of serving as the dean of a School for Local Pastors, which is a basic training course that our denomination provides for beginning pastors. I was amazed at the variety of people who registered for that school. Some were beginners who had little education beyond high school and no experience except that which they had had in their home churches. Others were seminary students, one was a seminary graduate, and one had a Ph.D. in another field. They had a great variety of different needs. In this book, I am going to give a very basic introduction to the pastor's role in pastoral care and also some practical directions about how to provide pastoral care. I will even get down to answering questions like *Where do I stand, and what do I say?* Much that is in this book will seem obvious and elementary to many readers. I ask your indulgence. Please remember that I am answering questions that some other readers may be asking.

I am happy to express my gratitude to the people who have contributed to this book's development: Peter Miller and Vicki Peters, who helped me find written resources; Ruby Nelson, Ray Nelson, and Bill Denham, who are pastors of small membership churches who read and critiqued my manuscript; Terrie Livaudais and the other people at Abingdon Press who have guided me through the process of preparing this book for publication; and my wife, Mada, who is my partner and helper in all that I do. I also want to thank all the church members and fellow pastors with whom I have shared life in ministry over the years. It is the experiences and insights that you have shared with me that make up the substance of this book.

1

An Opportunity
for Excellence

The Christian faith is about love. It is about God's love for
us. It is about God loving us into living in love. It is the
mission of the church to lead people and communities
into life-shaping relationships with God, who loves us. That
should be the subject of the proclamation and of the teaching of
the church. But the best way to lead people into a life-shaping
relationship with God is to invite them into a community in
which God's love is embodied in the relationships among people.
Bringing people into a community of caring believers and into
relationship with a caring pastor can enable people to experience
God's love in ways that can make a big difference in their lives.

Small membership churches have a real advantage when it
comes to incorporating people into a fellowship in which they are
known as persons and in which their personal needs are met.
Small churches and their pastors should not fail to make the most
of this ministry. They can excel in it. It can be the key to effectiveness in all the other ministries of the church.

In recent years, there has been a kind of preoccupation in
church circles with large membership churches and mega-
churches, as if those kinds of congregations were considered the
norm by which all churches are to be measured. It is true that a
large percentage of the people who are now active in churches

1

are served by large membership churches in urban centers. These churches have their unique mission and needs and problems and possibilities. But so do small membership churches.

The very demographic distribution of people in America, and in other places too, determines that, if everyone is to be served by the church, many will have to be served by churches with an average attendance of fewer than one hundred. Many of these are vital, active congregations in small towns or rural areas where there are just not enough people to make up a large church. Many of these churches will be served by part-time pastors or by "circuit-riding" pastors who serve more than one congregation. Some of these may be declining churches, which, for reasons beyond anyone's control, are smaller than they once were. These churches face some unique challenges.

It should be obvious that small membership churches play a needed and important role in the total mission of the church. The network of small membership churches that presently exists reaches into almost every town and community, even the most remote. When I drive across the country and see church signs with the symbol of my denomination on them in every little town and in some places that are not towns, I get really excited about the possibility that distribution of churches represents. Those churches, together with similar churches of sister denominations, have tremendous potential for meeting human needs, affecting the quality of life, and shaping the way of life in America and in many other places. It is not hard to see what role they can play in fulfilling the commission that Jesus gave to his disciples at the time of his ascension: "You will be my witnesses in Jerusalem, in all Judea and Samaria, and to the ends of the earth" (Acts 1:8).

Most pastors will spend some time, if not their whole careers, serving small membership churches. While you are the pastor of a small membership church, you will be wise to give that church your best. "Bloom where you are planted." Your own integrity as a person and your need for meaning in your life should require that. If you spend your whole life serving small membership churches and doing it well, yours will have been a life well spent. But even if you are destined to eventually serve large membership churches, the insights and experience you will gain while serving small membership churches will be priceless training to prepare you for leadership in larger congregations.

There is a notion rattling around in church circles now that every church ought to imitate all the things that mega-churches do. The assumption is made that doing those things will make any church grow. I have known some pastors who have gone off to conferences on church growth and come home believing that, since the senior pastors of mega-churches do not do much pastoral visitation, they shouldn't do visitation either. (Somehow they must have missed hearing how much energy effective large church pastors invest in seeing that their churches provide the kind of caring relatedness that comes naturally to small membership churches.)

Small membership churches are different from large churches in ways other than size. They are a different kind of organism. They live differently. They grow differently. Committed and creative pastors will seek ways of doing ministry that are appropriate and effective in their own church and community situations. Church growth can come to small churches in the same way that it should come to all churches, through people being led into life-shaping relationships with God, who loves us all.

Most laypeople in small membership churches want to have a personal relationship with their pastor. They want to know that their pastor knows them and cares about them and can be called on to minister to them. Soon after I arrived at my first pastoral appointment, one of the older church members, who wanted to be helpful, sought me out and said to me, "Folks up here like for the pastor to come around." He was letting me know that the church members would expect their pastor to initiate relationships with the people, to be a part of the community, and to be sensitive and responsive to the human and spiritual needs of the people. A pastor who opts out of that ministerial function may eventually hear the people saying, "Depart from me, you unfaithful and useless pastor, for I was in the hospital and you did not visit me; I was in grief and you did not comfort me; I was going through a bad time in my life but you did not seem to care about me."

Of course, the pastor should not be the only person in a congregation who is involved in caring ministries. The whole congregation should be a caring community. Being small gives a congregation a unique opportunity to be one, but small size alone will not make a church into a caring fellowship. That will take an intentional commitment on the part of the people. Each congregation should work at building up its network of caring relationships and its caring outreach to others. In that way, it can develop the ministry of its members and also meet the needs of its community.

There are usually some laymembers in every church who just naturally gravitate toward doing the work of caring ministry. But most churches will need for their pastors to give leadership in developing these ministries. They will need for the pastor to prepare people to respond to needs by providing both training and example. They will need for the pastor to know where the needs are and to help caring people to get in touch with the people who have those needs. They will need for the pastor to mobilize a comprehensive response to human needs. All these things are entirely possible for small membership churches and their pastors—and they will provide a rich and satisfying experience in ministry.

This book is based on three convictions: first, that small membership churches have an important role to play in the total mission of the church universal; second, that small membership churches have some unique and exciting possibilities for ministry that ought to be maximized; and third, that every pastoral assignment is important and deserves the very best, most faithful, and most creative service that its pastor can give it. Let's explore the possibilities.

For further study

Trebilcock, Robin. *The Small Church at Large*. Nashville: Abingdon Press, 2003.

Pappas, Anthony G., editor. *Inside the Small Church*. Bethesda, MD: Alban Institute, 2002.

2

Moving into Relationship

The first step in offering pastoral care is moving into relationship with others. You must take the initiative in offering a special kind of friendship. You must get to know others, allow yourself to be known by others, and offer to become involved with others in certain significant ways. In a small membership church, you can and should offer that kind of relatedness to every member of the congregation and also to as many other people as possible in the community that the congregation serves.

This will come easily for some who are naturally gregarious and outgoing people. They will find it natural to reach out and to relate to others. But some are, by inclination, more private people who find it difficult to relate to others. Whether it is easy or difficult for you, moving into relationship with others is essential for effective pastoral care. You will have to work at that very intentionally.

There are certain external things you can do, certain motions you can go through, to dramatize your willingness to relate and to actually give relationships an opportunity to develop. Get out of the study one or two mornings a week and visit around the town square—if you live in a town with a square. Attend school carnivals and high school football games, whether or not you have children, and talk to as many people as you can. Attend community events, even fund-raisers at the other churches. Frequent the places where people go for coffee and speak to everyone whose eyes meet yours. When you are at a meeting or a community event, work your way around the gathering and speak to as many people as you can. You take the initiative. Don't wait for others to come and introduce themselves to you. Eventually, a trip to the grocery store will become a time for pastoral visitation. Later, I will suggest a systematic visitation of the whole congregation. These are all effective ways of announcing that you want to get to know people and of giving it a chance to happen.

These external actions can be helpful. But the kind of moving into relationship that really needs to occur is something that happens inside of you. It is something inside of you that allows something to happen inside of others so that significant interactions can take place between you. It starts with being genuinely interested in the people whom you serve, getting to know them, getting to like them and to trust them as much as you can, getting to really care about what is going on in their lives. It then moves on to making an offer of a particular kind of friendship.

If you happen to be a naturally withdrawn and private person, you may have to push yourself out of your "comfort zone" to do this. But less outgoing people are not at a complete disadvantage. In fact, some naturally outgoing people may tend to form only superficial relationships. Some may be so aggressive that they tend to fill up the space in a relationship with themselves and not leave room for the other. If you intentionally open yourself to others but do not come on too strong, you may actually offer a kind of relationship with which many will be more comfortable.

What is needed is a relationship in which you as pastor offer to share your life with others and invite others to share their lives too. The relationship must make space for the other. It must make space for the other as the other actually is. Acceptance is very important. But you must not try to force a relationship upon another. In a rural community, you may have to deal with many others who are naturally private people. They will resist anything they regard as an intrusion. But if an offer of friendship is made, and if they can learn to trust the one who makes it, the offer will be appreciated and may eventually be accepted.

The pastor must take the initiative in offering relatedness and then wait for the other to respond. The waiting must include permission to reject the offer of friendship as well as permission to accept it. It should also include willingness to keep the offer open until the other is ready to enter into it.

Offering relatedness like this involves a certain amount of risk and vulnerability. That is an inevitable part of a significant relationship. There will always be those who will abuse an offer of friendship either to turn you into an errand boy or to involve you in some personal agenda that may not really be good. It will be necessary to establish certain boundaries to prevent that kind of abuse of the relationship. But the vulnerability that goes with caring, the risk of having to hurt with others and the risk of being hurt by others, is part of the price a person pays for getting significantly involved. God pays that price for getting involved with us. We must be willing to pay that price if we are to participate in the work that God is doing.

One of the greatest barriers that some of us have to overcome is the barrier of our own inner insecurity. That is a very subtle thing. You may not fully understand it yourself. You will probably not need to go through psychoanalysis to try to understand it. You would be better advised to spend time in those personal relationships and spiritual disciplines through which you can experience God's affirmation of yourself. Then you will need to intentionally push past your resistance to move out into relationship even if that moving out is initially uncomfortable. If your offer of relationship is accepted and returned, at least some of the time, you may find that you are able to move out of yourself more freely.

Remember that it is OK to be a little anxious. It is a healthy thing to know your limitations. Remember that all you can do is to give the best that you have to offer. Do that and trust that God will use your efforts to accomplish good things. We will eventually talk about how to recognize situations in which you are up against something that is beyond your capabilities and how to make a referral to someone who has the skills needed to deal with it. Remember that most of the people in your congregation and many of the people in the wider community actually want a relationship with the pastor. They will appreciate your offer of friendship.

Building personal relationships can prepare the way for pastoral counseling and other kinds of pastoral care. In a small membership congregation, it can also position the pastor to work effectively in other areas of pastoral work such as leadership and preaching (especially sermons that are relevant to people's needs and those dealing with those tough social and moral issues). It would be hard to overestimate the importance of building pastoral relationships in small membership churches.

Beginning ministers, especially young ones, are often eager to know what authority they have to make changes and to decide what will be done in the parish. That really is not the way things work in a church of any size, especially in a small church. Effective pastors lead. They do not command. You will need to work with people and to lead them into making needed changes and undertaking needed ministries. That kind of leadership becomes possible when people know and trust you and believe that you really want what is best for them and for their church. Much of that leading takes place not in the business meetings and not from the pulpit, but in the personal conversations that take place before the meetings. In those settings, the pastor is able to share ideas and to let people think about them and warm up to them. In those situations, you can also discipline your own thinking by listening to the feedback from church members and considering whether your ideas are really right for the church and whether the congregation is ready for them. In a small membership church, effective leadership grows out of effective pastoral relationships.

Leadership through change can be really crucial for many churches. Many small membership churches need to make important changes in their ways of doing things in order to survive and to minister effectively in a changing world. Most small membership churches resist change. Only a pastor who has won the trust of the congregation through building good pastoral relationships will have any chance to lead the churches through the needed changes.

Pastoral relationships also prepare the way for prophetic ministries. In every generation, there are some big issues that God wants preachers to talk about even though the congregations don't want to hear about them. That is part of the way God works through the church to change the world. I will always remember the 1960s when the Civil Rights movement was going on. Many of us felt that God was calling us to speak out on issues of justice and, if possible, to lead the churches into some loving action. Many churches *really* did not want to hear that. That one issue kept me in hot water for the first third of my ministry. Those of us who were able to speak or act on that issue and survive in our pastorates were the ones who had built good pastoral relationships with our people. We had learned to speak to them as to people God loves and wants to lead into a better life. We did not treat them like enemies of justice and condemn them. And those of us who had served the people by caring for them when they were sick and being their friend when they needed a friend, had built up a certain amount of "credit" with our congregations. That made them willing to tolerate a few ideas they didn't like and even to begin to think about them. God is not yet through trying to change the world. Prophetic ministry is still part of the pastor's mission. And effective pastoral relationships can help facilitate that.

But, apart from all that, building the kinds of relationships I have been describing can, in and of itself, carry much of the freight of Christian ministry. Such relationships communicate better than words ever could the forgiving, accepting, healing, and enabling love of God. Remember, that is what the work of the church is all about.

As you move into relatedness, you will become more and more comfortable in it. Relationships will grow and become an affirmation of your pastoral role. Your confidence in your ability to share significant pastoral relationships will grow.

Of course, you may find yourself up against some really bad situations in the lives of some people or in the life of some congregation that will prevent you from moving into significant pastoral relationships. These bad situations can come in an awesome variety of shapes. Remember that, if things don't work out, it is not always your fault. It is your responsibility to take the initiative and to make the offer. Do your best to make things better. It may become necessary for you to move on and start over in a new parish.

If in time you discover that you are never going to be able to effectively move into caring relationships, you would be wise to seek the counsel of someone whose wisdom and experience you respect and consider whether you should rethink your calling to pastoral ministry. Being a minister without building caring relationships simply is not possible, especially in small membership churches.

Your offers of pastoral relatedness will probably be welcomed, and you and your congregation will probably move into a kind of sharing of life that you will both find richly rewarding.

For further study

Haugk, Kenneth C. *Christian Caregiving: A Way of Life.* Minneapolis: Augsburg, 1984.

3

Learning the Art of Pastoral Conversation

Sometimes pastors are called on to do counseling. Sometimes someone will make an appointment with you and come to the study for a formal counseling session much as they would with a psychotherapist. You should do your best to develop the skills needed in that kind of situation. But, in fact, that kind of formal counseling may happen much less often than you might expect in small membership churches. In small churches, counseling is more likely to happen informally, while you are sitting with a church member on a front porch or in a hospital waiting room or at a table in the coffee shop. In settings like that, a person who has learned to trust you may bring up some deep feeling that needs to be shared or some troublesome problem with which he or she needs some help.

Always be sensitive to what is going on in conversations. Be alert to recognize the signs that a conversation has moved to a deeper level or that the other person in the conversation is checking to see if you are willing for the conversation to move to a deeper level. I learned to watch for those situations in personal conversation when a person gets a faraway look in his eyes and says, "Preacher, what do you think about . . . ?" or when someone tells a story about something that has happened in another person's life and wants my response. I have learned that those people are often either indirectly asking for help with their own problems or checking to see how I would respond before they share their own problems. When that happens, come to attention and proceed as if you are in a counseling session.

Later, I will talk about how to handle a formal counseling session. But now I am going to spend some time introducing you to some basic counseling skills. These skills will enable you to engage in a kind of conversation that will often be appropriate in many of the pastoral settings that we will discuss.

There is a limit to what we can accomplish by talking about counseling skills. Counseling is like golf. You don't learn it by reading a book about it. You learn it by doing it and reflecting on what has happened, preferably with the help of a skilled supervisor or "pro." Learning and improving counseling skills is something that you should work at throughout your career. Clinical Pastoral Education (C.P.E.) programs, which are offered through the chaplaincy programs of many major hospitals, are probably the best training that is readily available to most pastors. But there are a few things you can learn about counseling skills that will help you develop the art of pastoral conversation and prepare you to respond to needs that you will encounter. We will share them so that you can use them until you can get better training.

It is important at the start to get some clarity about the objective of pastoral conversation. The objective is to help people become whole persons who can live their lives freely and fully and meaningfully and who can finally solve their own problems. A perceptive reading of the stories of Jesus will show that he was trying to do that in all his interactions with the people to whom he ministered. Healing, very broadly defined, was his objective. In fact, the Greek word that Bible scholars usually translate "to be saved" actually originally meant "to be made whole." Jesus went about doing this healing work in many different ways that were appropriate for the unique needs of the different people with whom he worked. If Jesus worked to make people whole, so should we. A similar thing could be said about trying to build healthy group life in families or congregations or communities. Relationships often need to be healed or built up.

If wholeness is the objective, then the methods we choose ought always to serve that objective. No approach that would tend to make another person dependent would be appropriate. Instead, we should choose methods that work to free other people and to enable them to solve their own problems. Beginning pastors are often overwhelmed by the idea that they must know how to give advice that will solve everyone's problems. That really is not what needs to happen in a counseling relationship. Instead, seek to relate to other people in ways that will help them grow in their freedom and in their ability to put their own lives together in ways that will make them work. Well, how might you do that? Here are some suggestions.

Affirm the personhood of the one with whom you are working. That can be done in nonverbal ways. Shake hands warmly. Face the person and maintain eye contact throughout the conversation. Don't allow yourself to be distracted or to give the impression that you are preoccupied with something else. Learn the person's name. Express a genuine interest in what he or she thinks about some relevant subject. All these ways of communicating tell the other person, "I recognize you as another person like myself and I respect you."

Acceptance is another important part of building a helpful relationship. Many people suspect that other people, especially pastors, may find something about them objectionable. They feel shut out from the beginning. It is important to communicate respect and openness in spite of whatever the other person may think would interfere with it. Acceptance is not the same as approval. Sometimes, when some moral matter is involved, you may have to find ways of communicating that a person is accepted as a person even though you cannot approve of some aspect of the person's behavior. But it is often not a moral issue that stands in the way. Some people may feel that they are unacceptable because they are poor, or because they lack education or cultural sophistication, or because they work at a job that requires them to get dirty. You must communicate that none of these things is a barrier to relationship. Again, this is best done nonverbally.

Also communicate openness, an availability to the other, and a willingness to get involved. If you have good reason to suspect that willingness to get involved might be exploited or abused, it may be necessary to define the kind of involvement that is being offered and its limits. That can be done subtly and politely. Being open to others may require you to share something of your own life and to be honest about your own humanity. It would be a mistake to burden others with your own confessions, but it is necessary to let the other know that you know you are human too. Unless you communicate a genuine openness to another person and to what is going on in that person's life, no significant pastoral interactions are likely to take place.

In a small community, you can come to be known as an affirming, accepting, and open person through day-to-day relationships with people. When that happens, people are likely to seek you out for helpful interactions.

At some point in a relationship, you may feel called upon to offer some caring involvement. It is important to know how to offer involvement without intruding. There must always be an invitation and a waiting to see if the invitation will be accepted. This is one of the most important skills a pastor can develop. If you are the pastor of the church in which a person has membership, you may assume that you have a certain level of entrée into that person's life. You can assume, unless you have reason to believe otherwise, that you can initiate a relationship by making a get-acquainted call. You can visit a person if he or she is in the hospital. You can make a sympathy call if there is grief. But when you move into such a relationship, pay close attention to how much the person wants to talk and what the limitations of his or her readiness to share may be. If you believe that some church member has a special need for a helping relationship, you, as pastor, may find some way of making yourself available to that person. But leave it to the person to decide whether to tell you about the need or to invite you to get involved. Offer but do not intrude. Even at very advanced levels of counseling, a skilled counselor will be constantly trying to gauge how much the counselee is willing to share and how open he or she may be for the counselor to be involved. The counselor must wait for the invitation.

If a person does invite you into some helping involvement in his or her life, the first thing to do is to listen, listen, listen. Try to understand what is going on in the life of the other and to appreciate his or her feelings. Pay close attention to everything that is said. Pay attention also to the nonverbal communications, the feeling tones, the body language, and the things that are left unsaid. Try hard to understand what the person is trying to share with you. Let the person know you are trying hard.

Reflective responses can be helpful. These are little responses that you can make from time to time during the conversation to let the person know that you are still with him or her. Sometimes brief summaries of what you have heard can be a helpful kind of feedback. You might say something like: "I hear you saying that . . ." or "Do I understand you to be saying . . . ?" or "It sounds to me like you are feeling. . . ." Not only do these responses assure the person that you are with him or her, they also give you an opportunity to check to see if you are understanding what is being said. Surprisingly, reflective responses can also help the speaker hear what he or she is saying. Persons in counseling may not completely realize what they are thinking or feeling until another person feeds it back to them. That may help them gain self-understanding and reflect critically and constructively on their own thoughts and feelings.

Sometimes active listening alone will meet the other person's need. I recall one occasion on which a person came to my study for a formal counseling session. The person shared one problem after another. I listened and made reflective responses. As I became more and more aware of the complexity of the person's situation, I began to worry about how I should proceed. How could I possibly help this person unravel all those problems? Then, just as I was about to give up and recommend a referral, the person terminated the conversation by standing up and saying, "Pastor, I just can't tell you how much you have helped me. Thank you ever so much." I have known other pastors who reported similar experiences. You don't have to control the solution to a person's problems. You don't even have to know what the solution will be. You are only called to help the person find a solution.

15

Listening skills are some of the most important skills you can develop. It is important to keep listening. One of the most unhelpful things you can do is to take the initiative away from the other and start telling about your own experiences or covering the person up with advice. Keep listening.

If a person shares a problem with you and asks for your help, it is your job to help the person find his or her own solution. This is best done by listening, reflecting on what you are hearing, then trying to help the person think the problem through. In that process, you can help the person define the problem, identify all the possible solutions that are available, and evaluate those solutions. It is the responsibility of the person who owns the problem to choose one of the available solutions and to act on it.

If the problem being discussed relates to a religious or moral issue, it is appropriate for you to share your convictions as *your* convictions or to explain the teachings of the church. That may help the person get the problem into perspective. But the person must still think through to a solution that will be his or her own. For example, if someone is talking with you about whether or not to have an abortion, it is appropriate for you to explain your church's teachings on the subject and also to share your own convictions. But you would not be wise to try to compel the person to act on the basis of your convictions. If that should happen, the person involved, or the families, or you yourself might eventually come to hold you responsible for the results of those actions—and those results could be long-lasting and very serious. It must be made clear that the persons most directly involved in any problem situation must make their own decisions, own those decisions as their own, and act on them.

It is appropriate for you to bring the resources of the Christian faith to bear upon the situation of the person with whom you are working. You are the pastor. But there are good and not so good ways of doing that. Quoting scriptures in a negative and judgmental way is neither helpful nor attractive. Neither is quoting easy platitudes when some big problem needs more serious attention. Wait until you have listened long enough to begin to understand the real dynamics of what is going on in the situation. Then share any aspect of the Christian faith that you think may be helpful. Help the ones with whom you are working to understand what you are talking about. Offer a passage of scripture that they may want to look into. And leave them to deal with the suggestion you have made. If they ask you to go further into the subject with them, do so. See where the conversation leads you.

You will often find yourself in a situation in which a prayer will be appropriate. Sometimes it will be expected. In those situations, gather up as much as you can of the situation as you understand it and lift it up to the Lord. By doing so, we affirm that the Lord will understand and accept. Then, if it is clear to you what the people present should pray for—healing, comfort, guidance, courage—pray for it. If it is not clear what is needed, ask God to guide and enable the people as they move through whatever is ahead of them. Don't forget the prayers of praise and thanksgiving. They can do a lot of good. (Kenneth Haugk gives some helpful guidance on the uses of prayer and scripture in chapters 12–14 of the book recommended at the end of the previous chapter.)

You will eventually encounter people who have already got their minds made up about what they want to do and just want you to tell them that they are right. You will also encounter people who think they know exactly what it will take to solve their problem and they want you to solve it for them, often by giving them some money. These may actually be abuses of your counseling relationship—or they may not. When someone is abusing your concern, it is to that person's advantage for you to kindly help them see what they are doing and for you to help them assume responsibility for their lives. That is seldom easy to do.

Sometimes you will encounter someone who is about to do something that is clearly hurtful to self or to others, something that is really wrong, and who wants your support in doing it. Then it may be necessary to respond in a confrontational way, to make it very clear to that person that you believe what they are proposing is wrong and to push them to reckon with the wrongness of it. It is surprising what some people can rationalize. And you may be surprised that they may claim your tacit approval if you do not make it very clear that you do not approve. Confrontation is a counseling strategy of last resort. Sometimes it is needed. But if it does not work, it will probably end the relationship.

Sometimes you may be asked to help members of a family or a group to work out conflicts between them. Again, it is important to start by listening and reflecting. Help the people open lines of communication between themselves. Try to help each member hear and appreciate what the others are saying. Again, reflective questions may be helpful: "I think I hear you saying . . ." "Is that really what you are trying to say?" "Do you understand that your partner is feeling . . . ?" "Can we agree on what the problem is?" "Can we work together to make a list of possible solutions?" "Let's hear how each of you feels about each of these possibilities." Again, it is your role as counselor to facilitate communication and to help people work out their own solutions to problems.

In situations where some conflict is being resolved, it is very important for each person involved to believe that his or her opinion has been heard and taken seriously. A person cannot expect always to get his or her way. But each person has a right to believe that he or she had been taken seriously as a person and that his or her suggestions have been considered. That is especially true if the pastor is one of the parties involved in the conflict. (Yes, that sometimes happens.) We will think some more about conflict resolution later.

I hope all of this has not been overwhelming to you. Remember that no one is entirely adequate for this task. You will soon realize that you need to keep building your counseling skills. Remember that you can refer people who have needs that are beyond your capabilities to other helping professionals or agencies that have the needed capabilities.

As we go on, I will have more to say about the specifics of different care-giving situations. I have shared these basic techniques at this time because they will be useful in many different kinds of pastoral settings.

For further study

Dayringer, Richard. *The Heart of Pastoral Counseling: Healing Through Relationship.* New York: Hawthorne Press, 1998.

4

Making Get-acquainted Visits

I can remember how overwhelming it was to move into a community where I had never been before, a community of strangers, knowing that I had to become their pastor. Where should I start? Do you know that experience? One of the best ways for a pastor to move into relationship with the members of a congregation and a community is to make a get-acquainted visit with each church member family. Most church members will welcome a visit from their pastor. A visit with a family in their home can do a lot to help you get to know the family members and begin building a caring relationship with them. You can get off to a good start in a new parish by making a systematic series of visits to as many families as possible.

This visitation can serve a number of purposes. These purposes should be kept in mind. The visits can communicate to the people that you are genuinely interested in them and want to have a personal relationship with every member of the congregation. It can be the first step in building those relationships. It can also help you get an understanding of who the people are and what is going on in their lives. That will enable you to plan your own personal ministry and preaching. It will also give insights that will be valuable in planning church programs.

There was a time in many rural parishes when people were happy for the pastor to drop around unannounced at any time. It is best not to assume that is the case any longer. It would be wise to make an appointment before going for a visit. It would also be wise to make those appointments in a way that will allow any who really don't want a visit or who would prefer to visit somewhere other than in their home to express that preference without appearing to be ungracious. It would also be best to arrange visits with single people of the opposite sex who are near your own age somewhere other than in their homes. I will talk more about the reasons for that later. Many of these problems can be solved by thinking through the logistics of the visitation program and making a plan.

It is best to announce your plans for visitation to the congregation from the pulpit or in the church newsletter if you have one. As a new pastor, you may choose to send a letter to every member introducing yourself and mentioning the plans for visitation. The members need to understand what you are planning and why you are coming around. Some may need to be set at ease concerning the nature of your visit.

An announcement of a plan for visitation might sound something like this: "I am really happy to have been chosen to be your new pastor. I am eager to get to know you all so that I can serve you as well as I can. Some time in the next few months, I hope to have a visit with each of you and your families just to get acquainted. I would be happy to come to your homes. If that isn't convenient for you, I would be happy to meet you at the church or at some other place that you might suggest. I don't want this to be a big, formal occasion. I don't want you to clean the house or bake a cake or get dressed up. I just want to drop around and spend half an hour getting acquainted with you. I hope your children can be there because I want to get acquainted with them too. I will need your help in planning a schedule of visits that will work for us all." You will need to make that announcement several times so that everyone will understand what you are doing when you call to ask for an appointment.

Then you need to make a plan for letting people help you schedule your visits. You might plan your schedule for the next two or three weeks and make a list of times when you could make a visit. You can fasten that list to a clipboard and pass it around in church right after making your announcement so that people can sign up for a time when they would like for you to visit. They might also be asked to give their phone numbers and directions to the place where they would like for the visit to take place. (In rural parishes, that can be rather complicated.) In doing that, you invite the people to invite you for a visit. That process may need to be repeated several times on successive Sundays.

You then need to follow up by phoning those who were not present when the list was passed or who did not sign up for a visit. "Hello, this is Pastor Jones. I am planning my schedule for get-acquainted visits and I am wondering if there is a time when it would be convenient for me to have a visit with you and your family." Be ready to suggest times when you might visit or to jot down times that they might suggest. Listen carefully to understand the response. Most will be eager to schedule a visit, but some may be busy and need for you to call back at another time. If, however, you get the impression that the person really may not want a visit, or, if you find them too busy several times, you might say, "We seem to be having a hard time getting together. I would still like to have a visit with you. Why don't you just look for a time that would be good for you and give me a call?" That leaves the offer open but allows the member to either schedule a visit or opt out graciously. If any of these people do call back, assume that they really do want a visit and work with them to arrange one.

When you go for your visit, be as warm and as friendly as you can. Dress professionally, whatever that means in the community you are serving, but don't dress up in a way that will make the people you are visiting feel uncomfortable. One pastor observed that it is important to sit down. Some people don't feel that they have had a visit unless you sit down. Ask get-acquainted questions concerning such things as the kinds of work the adults do, the grades the children are in and their activities, and how long they have lived in the community. Look around to see if there are things on display that may tell you about the family and their interests. Some of these things might be: significant family pictures, professional awards, little league trophies, hunting or fishing trophies, art work or other such things. If you see objects like that, comment on them and invite the people to tell you about them. Give the people opportunities to share what they want to share but do not pry into subjects that they do not offer. Be ready to share similar information about yourself, but keep the focus on the people you are visiting.

It can be helpful to ask some question about the church, like, "Which of the things that happen at the church is your favorite?" That can help you get some idea about the family's level of interest and involvement in the church. If refreshments are offered, the gracious thing to do is to take some. They may have been prepared especially for the occasion, even if you have suggested in your announcement that they were not expected. (However, think seriously about how much coffee you can consume and still keep visiting.) Do not stay too long. If you have mentioned thirty minutes in your announcement, you should stay as close as you can to that time. If you find yourself involved in a serious conversation that needs more time and you have another appointment scheduled, you may need to make plans to come back later and finish the conversation. If you see that you are going to be late for the next visit, phone ahead and revise your schedule. Some families may invite you and your spouse to come to their home or to a restaurant for a meal. Accept as many of these invitations as you can and allow more time for them. It is not polite to "eat and run."

After each visit, take some time to reflect upon what has happened. Make some notes. Jot down the names of the children and their hobbies so that you can show interest by asking about them later. Note the employers of the adults. Jot down any significant comments that may have been made about the church and their interest or lack of interest in any aspect of the church's life. Reflect on any feelings you may have gotten from the atmosphere in the family, the things that were communicated without being said, the evidence of any grief or conflict in the home, or the evidence that the family is excited about something that is happening in their lives. Consider whether or not you have learned about some needs that might helpfully be addressed in a sermon or through some church program.

Be realistic about planning your schedule. Allow an hour for each thirty-minute visit. Allow time for travel. If you are a city person serving in a rural community, you may find it geographically bewildering, and you will want to locate the places where you are going beforehand so you can find them when the time comes for your appointment. One pastor commented that it is awfully hard to find a mobile home at the end of the dirt road just beyond the big tree at night. Don't plan for more than three visits in a morning or an afternoon, or for more than two in an evening.

In many small membership churches, the get-acquainted visits may be accomplished in the first few weeks of a pastorate, but allow from three to six months so that those on whom you have not yet called will not feel left out. Realistically, you probably never will be able to visit every family. Some people will be very busy, and some will just not really want a visit. Look for other opportunities to build relationships with them. Give your best effort to your get-acquainted visits. You will find that they have done more than you could have expected to build caring relationships and to facilitate your ministry.

It is difficult but very important to build relationships with young people. Important things are going on in their lives, and they need a relationship with the church and a pastor. Some young people feel awkward about forming relationships with anyone outside of their peer group. They may not understand that any adult would really want to get to know them. It is best not to be too aggressive with young people, but you will probably have to take the initiative in establishing the relationship. Go where young people are. Get to know some of the young people in your church and let them be a bridge for getting to know their friends. Do this carefully so as not to make them feel conspicuous or awkward. If you can get to know young people so that you can greet them by name—"Hi, Billy. How is football practice going?"—you may be able to open some important doors.

I have begun all of my ministries except one by making a series of get-acquainted visits. I have found it very helpful. My last appointment was to a two-thousand-member church with several urgent situations that needed attention. I did not feel that I could accomplish an effective every-family visitation. I always regretted it. I never felt that I really knew the members of that church as I wanted to, or that I was in ministry to them as I wanted to be. I strongly recommend a systematic effort to get acquainted with everyone as an effective way to begin a ministry. In a small membership church, it should be entirely possible.

After your initial series of visits, you will probably know which of your members need further attention because of some need, which ones would be glad for you to "come around" as often as you have time to visit, and which ones really don't need much attention. Many of your future formal visits will probably be made for specific purposes: to ask someone to serve on a committee, to pay a sick call or a sympathy call, to talk about baptizing a baby. Your formal visitation can be supplemented with the informal contacts through which you will continue to build relationships. Moving into relationships can and should be a real joy.

5

Visiting Shut-ins

There is one group of people in every church who will need regular visitation from the pastor and other caring people from the congregation. These are the elderly or infirm people who are confined to their homes or to nursing homes. These people have lived long and useful lives. They may have once been committed leaders in the church. They may have lived quite remarkable lives and become very significant people in times past. But now they can't get around anymore. They may be suffering from painful physical afflictions. They may be suffering from grief over the loss of loved ones and over the loss of the lives they once had. They may be very lonely people. Each one is unique, just as every other person is unique. But now, because they cannot go to the church, they will need for the church to come to them.

This may not be your most pleasant duty. Sitting in an over-heated little house, smelling stale coffee and dust, trying to stay awake as you listen to someone tell you about his or her ailments may not be what you call a high aesthetic experience. And walking down a nursing home hall, smelling urine and disinfectant, past lines of people in wheelchairs, some slumped in uncomfortable sleep and some staring at you through eyes that betray the utter confusion of the minds behind them, can keep you mindful of the fragility of human life and human dignity. So, who told you that ministry would always be pleasant? These people are beloved children of God who are in need. You or those whom you love may eventually be like them. This visitation needs doing, and it's your job to do it. And, in fact, once you get into it, you may find this aspect of ministry moving you into some valuable relationships. You may get to know people whose accomplishments in the past and courage in facing their present will make them inspirations to you.

The shut-ins should be among the first people you visit after coming to a new parish. They need that visit so they will know that they have a pastor and that the pastor cares about them. Secretly, some of them are anticipating their own deaths and they do not want their funeral service to be conducted by a stranger. The shut-ins will be very happy to see the pastor. Their days are often long and empty. Their family members, even the most faithful and attentive ones, are busy and can't spend as much time with them as they need. In fact, some families are not as faithful as they should be. These people may be starving for human relationships.

Each shut-in is a unique person and you should start fresh, without any presuppositions, in building a relationship with each one. I remember one lady informing me that she was not hard of hearing. I had been making visits in a nursing home, and I was talking loudly because I had come to assume that the people there needed for me to do so. Each visit should be a unique occasion. Come to each one ready to be sensitive to what is going on in the person's life and responsive to his or her needs.

When you go to visit, knock on the door and wait to be invited in. (Sometimes it takes a little while for people to find their shoes or hide their snuff.) It is a good idea to start by introducing yourself each time until you are very sure that you will be recognized. Some older people forget easily and sometimes get confused. It makes it so much easier if you start by saying, "Good morning. This is Pastor Betty from your church, St. Paul's. I have come around to see how you are doing." That clarifies the agenda and sets the stage for the visit. Speak a little louder and clearly. Many older people *are* hard of hearing. Be pleasant and upbeat in your visiting. Most shut-ins need to be cheered up. They will want to know all about you and about what is happening in the church and the community. They will also want to tell you their stories. The most valuable thing you can do for shut-ins is to listen to their stories—even if you have to listen to the same stories over and over again. Your listening attributes value to their lives—and many of them are feeling terribly devalued. Besides that, you just may hear some pretty good stories. One of my first published writings was an article made up of stories old men had told me about pranks they had pulled when they were boys.

It is a good idea to have in mind a couple of happy news items to share when you come to make a visit. These may be about things happening in the church or community or in your life. Focus on things that will make the person feel good. Let the person you are visiting set the agenda.

Sometimes shut-ins may need some serious pastoral conversation. They may be dealing with things like grief over the loss of a loved one or grief and sometimes bitterness over the loss of their homes and the life that they once enjoyed. They may be involved in conflict with family members or with other people in the nursing home. They may be in pain because of deep disappointments over goals not achieved, physical suffering, and the anticipation of death. Some may be worried about things going on in the lives of family members or friends. When they have learned to trust you, they may share these things with you. Remember what you have learned about how to have a helpful conversation and do what you can. Listen, reflect, try to help them gain perspective. If there are scriptures you know that could be helpful, share them. These conversations can be deep and significant. Take them seriously.

Read a passage from the Bible as a part of the visit and share some devotional thoughts. Failing eyesight may keep shut-ins from reading the Bible for themselves. Close the visit with a prayer. Gather up all the concerns shared during the visit and lift them up to God with appropriate prayers of petition, intercession, and thanksgiving. Don't forget to do this. This is what you came for. You are the pastor.

One of the biggest problems in dealing with shut-ins is that they will need more caring than you will be able to give them. Some will try to get you on a schedule that may be too demanding for you to keep. If, on your first visit, the person says, "The last pastor came to see me twice a week," you will know what is happening. Be patient. She could actually use a visit twice a week. She is lonely. You will need to respond gently: "I will come to see you as often as I can, but I don't think I would have time to get all my other work done if I visited all the shut-ins twice a week." Be careful to time your visits so that they do not suggest a schedule. If you visit one shut-in on two successive Tuesday mornings, you can bet that she will be expecting you on the third Tuesday and will be disappointed and maybe even hurt if you do not show up. Be understanding. Try to involve other caring people in the church in ministry to shut-ins.

One of the saddest things that a pastor may have to deal with in visiting shut-ins is the loss of mental capacity that some of them suffer as a result of dementia or Alzheimer's disease. If you stay in a parish for a while, you will have to watch this happening to some people whom you have learned to love and admire. Some of us have a hard time dealing with that. It forces us to recognize just how delicately balanced human personhood really is. It also forces us to reckon with our own mortality. But the people suffering from these conditions are beloved children of God. They need and deserve the caring service of the church.

When you go to see people whose minds are failing, relate to them in terms of whatever capacity there is left. Analyze the possibilities present in each visit. They will change from time to time. Even when things start coming apart in a person's mind, there will still be flashes of memory and of recognition that ought to be evoked and related to. If a person has had a history of religious faith, they may not know who you are, but the concepts of "minister" and of "prayer" may still be meaningful. Relate to those bits of consciousness to enrich a moment of a person's life. Repeating the Lord's Prayer can sometimes evoke a meaningful memory. Some pastors continue to go by the rooms of people who have long since lost consciousness. They stand by the bedside and say a prayer. It is an intercessory prayer at the least, and it may stir some recognition in what is left of the person's consciousness. In this ministry, we are always working on the edge of mystery. You will have to make decisions in each case about how long it will be meaningful for you to continue a ministry of visitation.

Always be alert to recognize signs of neglect or abuse. Some shut-ins can be hard to deal with, and it may be easy for those who are responsible for their care to give in to their own fatigue or frustrations. When you see signs of neglect or abuse, report them to the family. If it is the family that has been neglectful or abusive, ask your local law enforcement officer whom you should report to. Love sometimes requires tough actions. But be careful about taking seriously the reports of neglect that come from a person whose mind is failing. One lonely little lady told me that her daughter had not been to see her in months. In fact, I learned that her daughter came every day and that she had just left an hour before I arrived. They just forget.

Ministering to people who are going through the disintegration of their lives or suffering from some cruel affliction can be very trying work. But these are persons of sacred worth. They deserve the caring ministries of the church. Mother Teresa of Calcutta would remind us that, in ministering to these people, we are actually ministering to Christ himself.

6

Ministering to the Sick

Jesus spent a great deal of his time and energy healing the sick. Church people who are suffering from illness will look to their pastors and their churches for something they need as they do the work of getting well.

Let's start with some brief reflections upon the theology of healing. This will provide a context for dealing with much more practical questions like, How do I make a hospital call? We can start with the belief that, even though we are mortal creatures and cannot live forever, God loves us and wants us to live as long as we can and to live as whole persons. Wholeness is a basic physical, mental, and spiritual health that will enable us to live lives that are full and good. Things like disease, injury, abuse, and mental and spiritual illnesses can limit our wholeness or even our lives. But there are healing powers that come from God at work in our physical bodies, in our mental and spiritual lives, and in the relationships of loving communities. These powers can work to move people toward wholeness.

Most Christians today take what has come to be known as a wholistic approach to healing—an approach that tries to mobilize the healing capacities of all aspects of a person's being to accomplish wholeness. When there is an illness or injury, we want the very best medical and surgical and mental health treatment that modern science can provide. They are gifts of God no less than are conspicuous miracles. We also want to mobilize the faith and love of the sick person and of the faith community. These can facilitate healing through the spiritual aspects of a person's life. We don't pray *instead* of going to the doctor. We go to the doctor *and* pray. As pastor, you can work effectively in situations in which healing is needed. You can act as the priestly agent of the love of God and of the faith community. You can also serve as counselor to help the sick person find a way of putting life together that can move the person toward wholeness.

There are many reasons for believing that this approach to healing actually works. Recent scientific studies have shown that people who are prayed for have a better chance of recovering from illnesses than people who are not. A group of ministers' wives who were all cancer patients or cancer survivors were talking one day. They shared a belief that they had a higher rate of recovery than many other cancer sufferers whom they knew. They agreed that they thought it was because they had been the beneficiaries of more loving prayers than many other people. They were profoundly grateful. Even in this secular age, many scientifically trained physicians and mental health professionals recognize the importance of the spiritual aspect of the healing process and value the work of pastors as part of the healing team. Most hospitals make provision for facilitating the work of pastors. As a pastor you will certainly want to do your best to play the role that medical science, your congregation, and God have assigned you in the process of healing.

I believe strongly that pastoral care of the sick is an important aspect of the pastor's work. I did not choose to specialize in pastoral care. When my doctoral studies required me to choose a major, I chose another field. But a desire to be responsive to the needs of people has caused me to spend so much time around hospitals that some people have thought I was a member of the staff. I have been on the other side of that ministry too. Late in my career, I spent seven weeks hovering around a hospital while my wife coped with a life-threatening combination of illnesses. I know firsthand how much the ministries of caring friends can mean.

How can you go about having a ministry to the sick? Illnesses come in a great variety, and so do the situations and dispositions of people who are ill. When you hear of a person who is sick, it is important to analyze the situation and decide what kind of ministry is needed. If a person has a case of influenza, he or she may just need to be left alone to wait out the healing process. If anything at all is needed from you, an encouraging phone call or a card will probably do. If there is a more serious illness or injury, you should make a visit to show the church's concern and to see what kind of ministry is called for. It is important to ascertain how the sick person perceives the illness and the need for ministry. If the sick person is anxious about the outcome of the illness, or suffering from serious discouragement or anger or some other spiritual malaise, you will need to do what you can to shepherd the sick person through that experience. When there is a serious illness or a prolonged hospitalization or confinement at home, you will need to come by frequently to continue to assure the person of the church's concern and to be available to offer ministry when it is needed.

You will need to discover some ways of learning when someone in your congregation is sick and needs care. Many people will expect you to know without their telling you. And many people in your congregation will just assume that you know. Many bad experiences can result from your not knowing. Remind your church members that clairvoyance is not one of the gifts of the Spirit. Let the people know that you would rather be told ten times that someone needs care than to risk not being told at all. You will soon discover that there are certain people in your congregation who know everything that happens in the community. Enlist those people to let you know when a church member or constituent is sick or hospitalized.

What are the rules and procedures for making a sick call? I will give directions for making a hospital call. You can modify this procedure easily for making visits in other settings. Some of these directions are going to seem obvious and unnecessary. Please be patient. There will be some who will need all of them.

Visit during hospital visiting hours if possible, even though most hospitals make provision for pastors to come at other times if they need to, especially if the patient is in an intensive care unit. In intensive care, visiting hours are usually short and strictly observed. If you come to an ICU at a time other than visiting hours, look for a hospital volunteer or an intercom at the door to the ward and check with the nurse on duty to see if it is convenient for you to come in. Unless there is some good reason for you not to come in, they will probably admit you for the visit. If they ask you to come back at a later time, understand that there must be a reason and respect their request. In hospitals, medical procedures must always take priority. If you are visiting a maternity patient, try to come during visiting hours. If you can't, check with the nurse on duty to see if it is all right for you to visit. If you are going to visit in a mental hospital or in the psychiatric ward of a hospital, check the day before going. You will need to see if your patient is allowed to have visitors and what procedures you will have to go through to be admitted.

When you come to the door of the patient's room, check to see if the nurse call light is on. If it is, ask at the nurses' desk if you may visit. If there is a "No Visitors" sign, again, go to the nurses' station, explain that you are the patient's pastor, and ask if you can visit. Often a pastor is one of the exceptions to a "no visitor" request. If there is a doctor in the room, or if there is a nurse performing any medical procedure more complicated than checking blood pressure, go get a cup of coffee and come back later. If the door is closed, knock and wait to be invited to enter. If there is no response, you may either open the door slightly and call the patient's name softly or go to the nurses' station to ask if you can visit. If a patient is sleeping, it is usually best not to disturb him or her. If for any reason you are not able to visit with the patient, leave a note written on one of your calling cards so the patient will know that he or she has been remembered. (By the way, calling cards are important in pastoral care. Have some made and keep some with you.)

When you enter a room, identify yourself. "Hi, I am Pastor Johnson from your church, St. Matthew's. I have come around to see how you are doing." Identify yourself even though you think the patient should know you. If a patient is sleepy or sedated or confused, he or she may not be able to recognize you immediately. You can make it easier just by introducing yourself. You never know what kind of conditions you will find in a hospital room. It is best to start out just being friendly, not somber, not bubbling with joviality. Go in ready for anything and try to assess the situation so that you will know what might be the most helpful thing for you to do. You may find a patient in pain, under sedation, depressed, disgruntled, needing to talk about some serious question, just needing company, or really needing to be left alone. It is all right to ask questions that will give the patient an opportunity to tell you about his or her condition. "When did you come into the hospital?" "Have you had surgery?" "How long do you expect to be in the hospital?" But it is best not to ask directly what the patient's condition is. Patients will tell you what they want to share with you.

It is difficult to give detailed directions for what to say and do in a sick call. The patient's needs will set the agenda. Use what you know about the art of pastoral conversation to make helpful responses.

During a hospital visit, it is best to stand by the bedside rather than to be seated. A patient lying in bed can see you better if you are standing. Don't stay too long. Five to ten minutes should be about the average length of your visit. If the patient has something he or she really wants to talk about, or if the patient is bored and just needs company, you may stay longer. But watch for signs of patient fatigue. If the patient is getting tired, promise to come back another time to finish the conversation—and keep your promise.

When it is time to go, ask the patient if you may say a prayer. Some pastors also suggest reading brief, relevant passages of scripture. The prayer should gather up all the concerns that have been shared during the visit and lift them up to God. It is appropriate to pray for the doctors and hospital staff and for the other patients in the hospital. If there is another patient in the room, include that person in the prayer whether or not he or she has been a participant in the conversation. Some pastors invite the patients to suggest what they would like to have included in the prayer. Do we pray for healing? We know that not all patients can get well. And yet we have been invited to pray for what we really need. Loving concern will cause you to earnestly desire healing. So, with the understanding that we can't always have all that we ask for, pray for healing. I will say more about that in the next chapter, on ministering to people who are terminally ill. When you pray, it is good to hold the patient's hand or to touch the patient on the arm or shoulder. There is sometimes healing in a touch. If there are family members present, they may want to join hands in a prayer circle. This prayer is an important part of the visit. Don't leave it out. You have come to represent God and the church and to be a channel for God's healing love. You have come to help the patient get in touch with the spiritual resources that can contribute to healing. If you are not sure whether or not a patient would like for you to pray, you might ask, "Is there anything I can do for you?"

How often should you call on a sick person? That depends on the need of the patient and the convenience in visiting. In a small town where the hospital is a few blocks from the church, it may be convenient for the pastor to visit every day, especially when a patient is seriously ill. It is best to avoid getting a reputation for visiting every day unless a patient is very sick. Keeping up such a reputation may become a problem. For most patients, a visit from the pastor three or four times a week will meet the need. Visits from other church members can be scheduled to add another dimension to the church's caring ministry. If the patient is in a hospital some distance from the parish, it may not be possible to visit frequently. But, even then, carefully timed visits should be made if at all possible. A visit before a patient leaves for the hospital, a visit at the time of surgery, and a visit at a time when the patient really needs it will be greatly appreciated. When the hospital is some distance from the parish, ask the hospital chaplain or another minister of your denomination who lives near the hospital to drop by and supplement your visitation.

Visits at the time of surgery are very important. Surgery can be a frightening experience at best. The chance that there may be unexpected complications or a discovery of malignancy adds to the anxiety most people feel when approaching surgery. Try to visit the patient on the day of surgery before the patient is taken into the operating suite. That may be difficult to do. You will need to become familiar with the procedures of each hospital. Most hospitals now have patients admitted on the day of surgery and taken to a holding area to await surgery. You can usually visit the patient there. If there is a staff chaplain at the hospital, she or he can tell you how to proceed. If there is no chaplain, ask the nurses in the surgery suite. Either scout this out on the day before the surgery or arrive early enough to find your way around. If you happen to be in the room when the nurse comes for the pre-operation examination, step out. Some of the questions that will be asked could be embarrassing.

A prayer before surgery is usually appreciated. Pray for the surgeon and for the surgical team. Pray for the success of the operation. Pray for the recovery of the patient. Pray for the family members who are standing by. Many pastors stay with the family members during the surgery. This is especially important if you know there may be extraordinary danger related to the surgery, if the family members seem especially anxious, or if only one family member is keeping watch alone. If you stay with the family, it is best to stay until the doctor comes out after surgery to make the report. Quite often, the family will be ready for another prayer after receiving the report. This may be a prayer of thanksgiving or, if the report is not good, a prayer lifting up to God the family's anxiety or grief and their prayers for guidance or for help. If you have not stayed with the family during the surgery, it is good to come back after surgery to inquire how the patient is and to share an appropriate prayer at that time.

When a church member is suffering from a prolonged illness, plan a regular schedule of visitation. Weekly visits, or visits on some other schedule that you can manage, will be appreciated. It will also be helpful to arrange for other church members to visit and to offer needed services. A person who is going through a long ordeal should not ever think that the pastor or church has forgotten.

People suffering from mental illness present some special problems. It is important for a pastor to treat people who are mentally ill as much like other sick people as possible. The patient and the family may feel that there is some stigma attached to being mentally ill. The pastor and the church should act in ways that will dispel that feeling rather than reinforcing it. As we have already observed, visiting in a mental hospital presents unique challenges. But it is important to visit as often as possible. If the patient is under the care of a psychiatrist or other mental health professional, it is imperative that the pastor not get involved in any counseling activity that might appear to contradict or complicate what the doctors are doing. Be supportive of the patient. Be supportive of the mental health professionals who are treating the patient. And bring the spiritual resources of the faith into the service of the healing processes.

A church can enlarge and deepen its ministry to the sick by involving trained lay caregivers in visitation and other ministries. I will say more about that later, in the discussion about mobilizing the whole congregation for caring ministries.

Some churches, as a part of their ministry to the sick, plan regular services of healing. These are not the spectacular kinds of services often associated with faith healers. They are warm, loving occasions when people come together to pray for those who have special needs. Many churches provide rituals for such services. The sacrament of the Lord's Supper is frequently included. People are invited to kneel and ask for prayers for wholeness. Physical healing is not the only kind of need that is lifted up. Then the pastor and other caring people may lay hands on the people requesting prayer and pray for them. Many people find these services very meaningful.

For further study

Kirkindoll, Michael L. *The Hospital Visit: A Pastor's Guide.* Nashville: Abingdon Press, 2001. This book shares many helpful experiences of the author.

7

Ministering to the Terminally Ill

Ministering to someone who is dying is one of the greatest challenges of pastoral ministry. It is a challenge that you will probably have to meet much sooner than you think. It may be waiting for you when you arrive at your first parish. People die. Sometimes the process of dying is stretched out over many months or even several years. Cancer is one of the enemies that can put a person through that ordeal. There are others. Terminal illnesses are those which a person lives with for some time, sometimes a long time, knowing that they cannot get well and that death will come at some predictable time in the not too distant future.

A person who is living through the process of dying will have many physical and spiritual battles to fight. If the dying person is a person of faith, or has any openness at all to the resources of religious faith, she or he may want and value highly the ministries of a caring pastor and a caring congregation during their lonely and painful time. Some of my most meaningful memories of ministry are of times when I was called on to walk with someone I loved through the valley of the shadow of death.

The outward motions of ministry to persons who are terminally ill are much like those of other kinds of pastoral care. You will need to make get-acquainted visits, informal contacts, hospital calls, and surgery visits so that your relationship with the dying person can develop and change to meet the person's changing needs as the illness progresses.

The greatest challenge involved in ministering to people who are terminally ill is the inner challenge. First you must come to terms with your own mortality so that you will be free to deal with the reality of death. That requires some serious growing for most of us. Then you will need to be intentionally present and sensitive to what is going on in the life of the person to whom you are ministering. She or he may go through different stages and have different experiences and needs at each of these stages. You will need to be sensitive to what is going on in the life of the patient and be ready to respond to these needs as they develop.

Most of us have ways of putting death out of our minds because we don't want to deal with it—or because we are not able to deal with it. When you first saw the title of this chapter, were you tempted to skip it, thinking that it is certainly something you won't have to deal with for a long time? When patients receive the news or come to the consciousness that they are going to die (patients often know before their doctors do), they may want to talk about it with the people whom they love. They need the support and the help in coming to grips with their situation that significant conversation could give. But the typical response of well-meaning friends and family members is, "Oh, no! Don't talk like that! You're going to get well." When a dying person hears that response, he or she takes it to mean, "I can't deal with what is happening to you. You will have to go it alone." And then the dying person may feel very lonely. When someone wants to talk to you about dying, unless you have some very good reason to believe that the conversation would be inappropriate, be open to what the person wants to say to you. Hear his or her concerns. Talk as openly and comfortably as you can about the possibility of dying. Someday we are all going to have to come to terms with the reality of death. And don't be too quick to give pat answers about going to heaven. There will be a time to talk about that. But if it comes too quickly or too easily, the patient may take that as another way of saying that you don't want to hear about his or her feelings or to share the experience.

I remember a hospital visit in which the patient asked his family members to step outside so he could talk to me alone. He then told me that his doctor had told him he did not have long to live. He said that his family had not been able to accept that fact. He needed for me to know. I responded by saying, in effect, "I hear what you are saying to me, and I want to be as helpful to you as I can in the time to come. I will be visiting you from time to time. We can talk about anything you want to talk about, but we don't have to talk about anything unless you want to talk about it. When I come around, you can know that I know what your condition is and I will be praying for you." I continued to visit several times a week. He never brought up the subject of his dying again until near the last. But knowing that I knew and accepted and cared seemed very important to him.

Some people have many things they need to talk about. They may have different things that they need to talk about at different times in their dying. Elisabeth Kübler-Ross wrote a definitive study on death and dying. She explained that people going through the process of dying go through certain stages. Not all people go through all the stages, and not everyone goes through them in the same order. But each stage calls for certain responses from the caregivers. Let's review these stages and see if we can imagine how we might need to respond to someone who is going through them.

The first stage in dying may be denial. A person in denial simply refuses to believe that the doctor's diagnosis is true. He or she may even refuse needed medical treatment. There is a great difference between denial and holding on to hope and working at getting well. There are many people (including my wife) who have hung in there and gotten well even after it had appeared that they could not. Caring friends will certainly want to support the courageous efforts of people who know that they are dealing with a potentially life-threatening illness. It is possible for a patient and his or her caregivers to be both fighting for recovery and coming to terms with the likelihood of death at the same time. One of the most difficult things I have had to do when pastoring a dying person is to know when it is time to stop praying for healing and to start praying other kinds of prayers. One pastor, who was himself in remission from a terminal kind of cancer, observed that God always heals. God sometimes heals by medicine, sometimes by miracle, and sometimes by death. In the context of the Christian hope, death can be seen as a kind of healing. This kind of understanding can help a person come to terms with the reality of a terminal illness.

The second stage that Kübler-Ross identified is anger. Many of us have a hard time dealing with anger. We think that nice people don't get angry. But some anger is appropriate and healthy in response to things that are really hurtful, either to yourself or to others. The anger of a person who has just learned that she or he is about to lose everything in death is understandable. It can, however, get misdirected. The dying person may vent that anger on the doctor, the hospital staff, the family, the pastor—even on God. Pastors and friends are wise to accept that anger as legitimate and to help the angry person focus it where it belongs, on the illness and on the situation rather than on people. Don't feel that you have to defend God against a dying person's anger. God can handle it. Just keep on loving the person who is dying and trying to appreciate his or her feelings. In time, the relationships with the doctor and the family will recover—and so will the relationship with God.

Sometimes the stage of anger is followed by a stage of bargaining. The patient begins to think, *Maybe if I do this or that the sickness will go away.* Sometimes this can take a religious form. People may promise God that they will do certain things if God will give healing. That is not a healthy form of spirituality. Pastors and friends should not encourage it.

When all of these attempts to avoid reality have failed and the patient has been forced to realize that he or she is going to die, deep depression may follow. Again, those who love the patient will need to be able to understand and accept these feelings. At this time, it is important to try to help a patient get in touch with the Christian hope. When time is slipping away, it is important to get in touch with eternity. The witness of the scriptures and of the Christian faith can help. Prayer can become very real and important. Psalm 22, which Jesus remembered as he was dying, can help a person understand that others have gone through the dark experience that she or he is having. Psalm 130, Psalm 23, John 14, 1 Corinthians 15, and Romans 8:31-39 might be helpful. Pastors and friends should work to help dying people move through the experience of depression to the next stages. Depression is not something from which you can back away. It has to be moved through.

Kübler-Ross identified the next stage as that of acceptance, the realization that life will soon be over and that, while one may not be happy about that, it is OK. The person who has come to acceptance may use the time that is left to attend to needed business; to work through unresolved conflicts, to say "thank yous" and "I'm sorrys" and "I love yous" that have been needing to be said, to enjoy the beauty and goodness of the life that is left, and to make the most of time shared with people she or he loves. This really is a matter of coming to terms with ones mortality. People who are going through this experience can teach the rest of us an important lesson. Life is not to be taken for granted or wasted on things that are really not important. Every moment of life is a precious gift that should be received gratefully, valued highly, enjoyed deeply, and used well. That lesson may well be the reward of those who love another through the process of dying. Once you have gained it, don't let it go.

Kübler-Ross said that the last stage of dying is a recovery of hope. This can be a recovery of hope for the future of the loved ones and of the world that the dying person is about to leave behind. Or it may be a recovery of hope for self that reaches beyond this life. The Christian faith can sometimes emerge triumphant in this stage of dying in a way that will be an inspiration to others who witness it. Pastors and friends should not try to force that experience on a dying person. But when it comes, and to whatever extent and in whatever way it comes, it should be celebrated.

Sometimes people demonstrate that they have come to terms with their mortality in surprising ways. Two officers of a credit union went to visit another of the officers who was in the hospital and not expected to live very long. The sick man explained to his friends that he knew he had only a few weeks to live. The two friends were quiet for a minute, then one of them said one of those things that we all say when we don't know what to say. "Is there anything we can do for you?" The dying man said, "As a matter of fact there is something you can do. Bring me a loan application." The two visitors looked at him with puzzled looks on their faces. Then they remembered that all of their credit union loans were insured and they all broke into laughter that was very hard for the floor nurse to understand. The man had come to terms with his own death.

It is important to emphasize that not everyone who is dying moves through all of these stages in exactly the order in which they have been described here. They may not have time to work all of these things through. The experiences that Kübler-Ross described can be all jumbled together. Or a person may slip back and forth from one stage to another. The thing you must remember is that many important things are being worked through in the life of a person who is dying. Work at being sensitive to all the things that are going on in the life of the dying person and think carefully about how you can best respond to be helpful.

A word needs to be said in this context about Hospice. Hospice is an agency that has emerged in recent years to help people come to terms with death and to give needed services to families that are caring for a dying relative. They give valuable service, and they will be eager to incorporate the work of the pastor and of the church into their work. It is a good idea to form a relationship with hospice agencies in your community so you can tell people who need to know about them at the proper time and so you can work effectively with them.

Does the prospect of having to be involved in the experience of the dying of a church member or of someone you love frighten you? It should. It is a very demanding and challenging task. It will require of you all that you have to offer and more. But take courage and venture on into the relationship when you are called to. Turn to God to supply the resources you will need. You will emerge from this ministry a bigger person than you were when you went in, and you will have answered the call of God to love those whom God loves.

For further study

Kübler-Ross, Elisabeth. *On Death and Dying*. New York: Macmillan, 1969.

8

Ministering to People Who Are Grieving

When you receive word that a member of one of your church families has died, or that one of the members or constituents of your church has lost a parent, a spouse, a child, or a good friend, you as pastor and your church are called into a special kind of ministry. You are called to offer sympathy. Sympathy means "feeling with." What people are feeling in a time like that is grief. Grief is the emotional aspect of the experience of losing someone or something that has been an important part of the life of the grieving person. I remember the deaths of my parents. Both were so infirm that death came as a release from suffering. But, for me, their deaths were losses that changed the shape of my world. When people are going through grief, they are likely to turn to their church and to their pastor for comfort and help, even if they are not accustomed to turning to the church for anything else. Something special will be expected of you as a caring person and of the church as a caring community.

Death is not the only thing that can cause grief. Any significant loss can cause it. A divorce, children moving away, the loss of a loved home (even when moving to a "nicer" one), the loss of a career (even through a well-earned retirement), the loss of youth, or any other significant moving out of one stage of life into another can all be occasions for grief. A pastor may not be called on to offer formal ministries of sympathy in all of these situations. But while you are offering pastoral friendship to a person who is depressed, or in some other way going through "a bad time," you may come to realize that part of what the person is experiencing is an unrecognized grief because of the loss of something that has been a part of his or her life. People do a lot of grieving.

Granger Westberg, in his excellent little book *Good Grief*, has explained that people may go through certain recognizable stages of grief that are, in many ways, similar to the stages through which a dying person may go. The first stage may be an experience of shock. It is hard to believe that the loss has really happened. This shock may be especially prominent in the experience of people who have suffered the sudden tragic death of someone they love. There may be a release of emotions, tears. There may be feelings of depression and loneliness. There may be physical symptoms of distress. (In fact, it is becoming apparent that grief—especially prolonged, unresolved grief—may contribute to the causes of some serious physical illnesses.) A grieving person may become panicky. There may be feelings of guilt even when there is really nothing that the person ought to feel guilty about. Some may experience anger, hostility, and resentment. It may be difficult for a person in deep grief to return to normal activities. These experiences may or may not come in recognizable, successive stages. But any or all of them may be parts of the experience of a person going through grief. They are not abnormal or necessarily unhealthy so long as a person is able to move through them and to come out on the other side.

Westberg says that the resolution of grief comes when a person is able to recover hope and to finally accept what has happened, to affirm life, and to move on. It should be the role of the pastor and of the church to help people move through grief to a recovery of hope and a resumption of life. Helping a person come to a resolution of grief is a very important healing ministry of the church. Wholeness is involved here, not only at the end of the process in which hope and life are recovered, but also during the process when a person is coping with what has happened. Grief is a part of life in its fullness. It is part of the cost of loving. Jesus said, "Blessed are those who mourn, for they will be comforted" (Matthew 5:4).

We will focus our attention on ways of ministering to a person or a family who is in grief because of a death. You can imagine ways in which similar ministries can be applied to other grief experiences.

When you hear that there has been a death in one of your church families, make a sympathy visit as soon as possible. Your visit will probably be expected, especially in a small membership church. If, for some reason, you are prevented from visiting immediately (you are away at school, you are sick, the family is in another city), then you should make contact by telephone as soon as you can. Express your sympathy and that of the church. Ask what can be done to meet the needs of those who are in grief. Plan to make a personal visit as soon as you can. This visit really should take priority over most of the other things in which you may be involved.

That first visit may be primarily a visit of caring presence, of just being there. (Learn the concept of caring presence. It is an important one.) The grieving people may still be in shock. The house may be full of friends and family members. You may not be able to do much counseling at that time. Seek out those who were closest to the one who died and those who seem to be experiencing the grief most deeply. Take their hand if possible, make eye contact and say a personal word of comfort. Just be there for a little while. That will be important. If you are to conduct the funeral, make an appointment with the family to come back and plan it. (We will talk more about the funeral in the next chapter.) It will usually be appropriate for you to ask all of those present to come together while you lead a prayer before leaving. You may also read a brief and helpful passage of scripture. The familiarity of Psalm 23 makes it a good choice for this occasion.

In future visits, try to understand what the grieving persons are experiencing and try to help them get through it. Some may need to be given permission to express their emotions. This may be especially true of men who have been taught from childhood that "big boys don't cry." They may need help in getting in touch with their emotions and permission to express them. There may also be some who think that a person of faith ought not to feel all of the things that they are feeling. They need to know that serenity comes at the end of the process of grieving, not at the beginning. Their pain simply means that they care deeply.

Grieving people need to talk. They need to talk about their own experience of grief. They may need to tell over and over the story of how their loved one died and of how they got the news and of what they felt and did at that time. You will do a great service by listening. They also need to be helped to talk about the person who has died. They may need to talk to you about that person, but, even more important, they need to learn to talk to one another about that person. They need to remember and reclaim the favorite times that they shared. They may need to remember that person's faults and any bad experiences as well as the good things. There is no need to dwell on these things, but it is important to be free to remember that they were there. It is good to remember the funny things that the deceased person said or did. It is not a healthy thing to avoid mentioning a person who has died for fear that the memory may cause some tears. Being able to talk comfortably about a person who has died is part of picking up the memories and moving on. If there are a few tears, that may just be because someone has not yet done his or her quota of crying. It is hard on a grieving person for others to act as if the one they loved never lived. Do a lot of listening. Encourage others to talk and listen to one another.

If you are the pastor who is to plan the funeral service, you can do many things in the planning process that will help people cope with grief. When I talk about the funeral sermon, I will talk about how to deal with some of the particular issues that may confront a grieving person.

The whole congregation should be involved in the caring response to grieving families. Small membership churches are especially good at this. In many communities, the women of the church customarily prepare a meal for the grieving family. In my first parish, the men were not comfortable showing their emotions or trying to use words to express them. It was the custom there for the men of the church to dig the grave. It was a beautiful custom. Laypeople who have received some training in caring ministries, can carry on the same kinds of ministries that the pastor offers. They can have a ministry of caring presence and of listening, and of making a witness to hope. In many small membership churches, the mechanisms for doing these things have been in place and functioning as long as anyone can remember. But if this is not so, the pastor should mobilize the church to have this kind of caring ministry.

It is important to remember that it takes a long time to move through the grief over a significant loss. There may be many caring people around during a funeral. But a few days later, they may all be gone. Then the grieving person may feel very lonely and in need of caring ministries. You and other church caregivers should remember to come around now and then for a while. Grieving persons may need systematic pastoral counseling for a while as they work through the grief. Some churches have sponsored grief support groups in which grieving people can minister to one another. A small membership church may be able to sponsor such a group as a service to the larger community. These can be very helpful. The anniversary of a death can be a very sad time for a grieving person. A call, a note, or a visit from a pastor or a caring friend can be very helpful at that time.

Grief does not go away quickly. Missing a person who has died may last a lifetime. But a person should be able to come to terms with the loss and take life up and move on within a year or two. If significant grief continues to inhibit wholeness and fullness of life after two years, a person may need some help from a skilled professional counselor. It is important to put caring arms around those who are grieving and just be with them.

For further study

Westberg, Granger. *Good Grief.* Philadelphia: Fortress Press, 1962.

9

Holding a Funeral

Holding funerals is a very important function of a caring pastor, one that is important to the family and the community. Funerals deserve your best.

There are three main purposes for a funeral: to give loving support to a grieving family and friends, to help those who grieve come to terms with death and gain a sense of closure, and to help people see the death of a loved one and their own grief in the light of the Christian hope.

Under ideal circumstances, funerals will take place in the context of your ongoing pastoral care of the congregation. Then you will probably be acquainted with the person who has died. You may have been caring for him or her through a long illness. You will also be acquainted with the family and friends. You may even have already helped the family plan the funeral. This will make you more effective in your ministry at the time of death.

You may, however, be called on to hold funerals for inactive church members whom you do not know or for people in the community where you serve who have no church affiliation. In these cases, do what you can to build helping relationships.

A funeral should be a ministry of an entire congregation to a bereaved family. There are many ways in which church members can be helpful. Plan ahead to facilitate these ministries.

Funerals take place in a cultural context. It is a good idea to inquire about local funeral customs. You may want to talk to your local funeral director about this. (It will be important for you to build a good relationship with him or her so you can work together effectively when the time comes to respond to a need.) The local customs will probably represent the family's expectations. Start there in planning your service and make variations in consultation with the family. If you have some strong—and different—opinions about how funerals ought to be conducted, share them with your church members in a class at the church, not while you are planning a funeral for some family's loved one. You may make suggestions, but the family's wishes should prevail.

When there is a death in your congregation, make a sympathy call as soon as possible. As pastor of the one who has died, you will probably be asked to hold the funeral. When members of your church lose a close family member or friend who is not a member of your church, make a sympathy call to your members. You may possibly want to attend the family visitation time or the funeral. But you should assume that the pastor of the one who has died will hold the funeral.

Determine as soon as possible who is actually to conduct the funeral service. Protocol calls for the pastor of the person who has died to do this. Often the funeral director will be the one who calls to inform you of the death, and he or she may tell you what role you are to play. Be sensitive that family members may have a close friend or favorite former pastor they may want to have lead or participate. You might facilitate this by saying, "I can hold the service for you or, if there is someone else that you would like to have come, I would be glad to contact him or her for you." In cases where a guest minister is invited, it is usually customary for the pastor to be the liturgist and the guest to preach the sermon. Let the family's wishes direct you.

The whole matter of former pastors or old friends coming back to hold funerals is very delicate. When you leave a parish, it is good to encourage the people of that parish to let their new pastor serve them by performing their weddings and funerals. You can come and participate just like any other caring friend. Don't let your ego get in the way of the ministry of the church. When an invitation comes from a family member or funeral director to conduct a funeral for someone who was a member of another church, it is best to get the pastor of that church involved. The invitation really should come from that pastor. The pastor will have a better chance of giving follow-up care. In unhappy cases where the family members don't like their pastor—or you—be as gracious as you can to all concerned. Give preference to the feelings of the grieving.

The funeral director will ordinarily contact you to see when the funeral will fit into your schedule. In the event that you are not accessible or time constraints make it necessary for the time to be set without your being consulted, do all you can to work with the schedule. Funerals of church members should take priority over most other commitments.

As soon as you can, arrange to meet with the family to plan the funeral service. This can be a very good occasion for coping and for healing. Invite the family members to share their favorite memories of the one who has died. This is good for them. It will also help you prepare the sermon, especially if you didn't know the person who died. Ask what the family has in mind for the service. I usually assure the family that the purpose of the service is to be helpful. If there is anything they think will be helpful, it can be done. If there is anything they think will not be helpful, they don't have to do it. Many are relieved to hear that. They may have some preferences, but they will need for you to give permission to express them. Some may want to opt out of some old traditional practices. Some may want to opt back into them. Ask if there are favorite hymns or scripture lessons that they want used. Ask if there will be some who should be asked to give personal tributes or if they want to give an opportunity to speak to anyone who wishes to do so. (In this last case, it will be best to have at least one person prepared to give the first tribute.) Take notes during this meeting and use them in your planning.

Determine the structure of the service. Compose an order of worship and give it to the funeral director. Determine when and where the service will be held, who will contact the musicians, who will contact the ushers, and who will prepare the funeral bulletin. It will be helpful to the family for the service to run smoothly.

Funeral services can follow many different formats. There may be a full worship service in the church with a traditional ritual followed by a processional to a cemetery and a graveside committal service. A modified version of that may be held in the church or at the funeral home. Or a simple graveside service may be held at the cemetery or mausoleum. Sometimes a memorial service or "Life Celebration" service may be held at the church or some other place for friends and all who want to come at a different time from a graveside service to which only family members and very close friends will come. It is nice for such a service to be followed by a reception at which friends can visit with the family members. The choice of a format for the funeral should be made on the basis of what the family thinks would be most helpful to them.

When a family has requested cremation, any of the kinds of services we have described can be held. This can be done with the body present before cremation or with the ashes present after cremation, or in the absence of either, perhaps with a photograph of the deceased on display. The family should, however, be encouraged to have some kind of memorial service. They will need it to help them gain closure.

Be open to the suggestions of the family. Most will prefer a shorter service. Most will prefer for the casket to be open for viewing and then closed when the service begins. However, some will still want the casket open during the service and will want the friends to pass by the casket after the service. Local traditions will be influential in such matters. Family members may not be able to tell you why they feel as they do about different aspects of the service, but their feelings are significant. Honor them.

The funeral sermon should take the unique situation of the grieving family and set it in the context of the Christian faith so that the resources of the faith can minister to the needs of the grieving. Remember and honor the person who has died. Make the service personal. Recognize and, if possible, respond to the feelings of those who are present at the service. Share the

Christian hope. There should be a scripturally based message that will be good news to those who are in attendance. Facilitate the work of the Holy Spirit as comforter.

It can sometimes be helpful to lighten up the occasion by some tasteful use of humor, preferably by sharing something humorous that the person who has died either said or did. One family that was planning their father's funeral went to great pains to tell their pastor all of the cantankerous things their father had done. They loved their father deeply. They loved him as he really was. He was a good man, but he was not a marble saint. They didn't want the pastor to preach a funeral sermon that would not rightly represent the man they loved.

Be sensitive to the unique needs that may be present in the situation. At the end of a long, well spent life, a funeral can be a celebration of victory. At the end of a long, painful illness, death may be thought of as a healing. When there is a premature or tragic death, assure the mourners that God is beside them mourning with them. Do not get caught up into assuring the people that "God took your loved one for some reason we can't understand." Many things happen that God doesn't want to happen. Harold Kushner addresses that issue well in his book *When Bad Things Happen to Good People*. Treat a suicide like any other tragic death. You will have to acknowledge the unique sadness of the occasion, but then assure the mourners that "[nothing] in all creation will be able to separate us from the love of God in Christ Jesus our Lord" (Romans 8:39), not even suicide.

When there is anger at the unfairness of the tragedy, honor it. Don't argue with it. The grieving people probably have a right to it. Pray for healing. When you sense that there are some guilt feelings floating around, address them indirectly. The mourners may not know why they are feeling them or even that they are feeling them. Maybe there are unfinished agendas for the relationship or unresolved conflicts. Some may feel that they should have been able to prevent the death or that they don't have a right to be alive while the other isn't or even just that they wish they could have done more. These are often not rational feelings and are not subject to rational remedies. But you can talk about how God's forgiving and healing grace works in our lives to give us back our tomorrow.

Sometimes you will have to deal with an unhappy situation in which there is conflict between the family members of the deceased. This can sometimes get really ugly. Try to do a work of reconciliation if you can. At least, try to keep the conflicting parties from doing anything that will make matters worse for the family in years to come.

When the person who died is not a Christian, don't make a judgment. Simply commend him or her to the care of the eternal God who loves us all. Some people may want and expect the pastor to say that the person has gone to heaven. This is customary in some denominations. Deal with that as tactfully as you can. Resist the temptation to preach an evangelistic sermon. It is inappropriate. Just hope that any non-Christians present will find the message of love and hope attractive.

Let the funeral service be a part of your larger caring ministry and that of your congregation to the family and the community in times of grief.

For further study

Mansell, John S. *The Funeral: A Pastor's Guide*. Nashville: Abingdon Press, 1998.

10

Weddings, Baptisms, Confirmations, and Other Occasions

As you have no doubt begun to realize, pastoral care is one aspect of many of the functions of a church and its clergy. Ministers get to participate in many of the joyful and deeply meaningful experiences of people's lives as well as the sad and difficult ones. Fortunately, the life of a pastor, taken as a whole, includes a healthy balance between the demanding experiences that keep us growing and the happy and inspiring experiences that can feed our spirits and enable us to rise to meet the challenges. You will get to share in many experiences that will make people smile when you see each other and remember. For the most part, weddings, baptisms or infant dedications, and confirmations are among the happy experiences of pastoral ministry. (Remember, I said "for the most part . . .".)

Weddings, baptisms, and confirmations take some of the happiest pivotal events in people's lives and set them in the context of the Christian faith. They dramatize the meaning and the possibilities of those events as interactions with God. They celebrate God's gifts of love, new life, and discipleship. They invite the participants to receive those gifts and to respond to the giver in a way that can make a real difference in their lives. Members of your church will expect you, as their pastor, to play a significant role in these events. And tradition will bring some who have drifted away from the church within your reach so that you can make a significant witness to the Christian faith and to what it can mean to them.

It will be important, however, for the church and the pastor to function on these occasions in a way that will maximize the life-shaping possibilities of the commitments involved and not just broker happy traditions that have lost much of their meaning for many. The church will need to define and publish policies that will establish that weddings, baptisms, and confirmations are important worship services of the church and are to be carried on in keeping with the teachings and traditions of the church and under the supervision, if not the direct leadership, of the pastor. These policies can go on to spell out just what things are and are not appropriate in each of these services. These policies should require at least one counseling session with the pastor in preparation for these events. Many churches require multiple counseling sessions or participation in classes designed to prepare couples for marriage or parents for the baptism of babies. One counseling session should be a minimum requirement.

The wedding service has three purposes. It should formalize a marriage contract. It should help a couple starting a new family to lay a foundation upon Christian beliefs, Christian values, and Christian commitments. It should allow friends and family to participate in a worshipful celebration of a loving relationship and of the beginning of a new family.

It is a beautiful thing when two people who share a vital Christian faith come to the church eager to start their life together with these purposes in mind. That should establish the context of a Christian wedding. But weddings like that are exceptional in our day.

You are more likely to find yourself dealing with two young adults who have drifted away from the church, or who never were in the church because their parents drifted away, and who have become thoroughly immersed in today's secular lifestyle but who, for the sake of beauty and tradition, want a "church" wedding.

You will encounter "search parties" made up of a future bride, her mother, and her best friend—most likely people you have never seen before—looking for a place to hold a wedding. They are looking for a church whose architecture they like and whose fees are not too high. The religious tradition of the church will not be important to them. Their attitude toward the church may range all the way from genuine reverence for the Christian faith and real good intentions to get involved in the church again someday, through tolerant indifference, to actual hostility ("I don't have any use for the church and all of its hypocrisies, but her mother insists that we be married in a church"). You may have to deal with romantic theatrics, social-climbing one-upmanship, and many other values imported from the secular world. These will, if they are allowed to, replace the Christian faith as the force that forms the event. The couple may already be living together and may already be expecting their first child. They may or may not share this information with you. They will not, however, feel guilty about it because it is perfectly acceptable in the culture of which they are a part. They will not appreciate your trying to make them feel guilty.

You will be wise to accept things as they are. Begin where the couple is, and, if you can, help them catch a vision of a better possibility. Take the wedding as an opportunity to help any who are willing to discover what the Christian faith has to offer that could help them build a really happy and lasting marriage. Your best opportunity to do this will be in the premarital counseling session. Many churches require several sessions of premarital counseling, complete with psychological profiles and sessions with professional marriage counselors. Still others require participation in classes for engaged couples. I admire those programs, but I have taken a more modest approach. I have customarily required one session—frankly, just because I have been able to make that requirement stick. Let me tell you how I have tried to make the most of that one session.

The purposes of premarital counseling are: (1) to give me an opportunity to establish a personal relationship with the couple, (2) to help the couple gain an understanding of the Christian concept of marriage and be ready to make the spiritual commitments required by it, (3) to deal with any problems that may need to be addressed as the couple prepares for marriage, and (4) to come to some agreement about the ritual (the choreography) of the wedding in preparation for the rehearsal. That is a full agenda for one hour.

I prepare the couple for the counseling session by giving or sending them three things. One is a copy of the approved rituals of the church. Another is a piece of literature about Christian marriage for them to study together. (*Growing Love in Christian Marriage* by Joan and Richard Hunt [Nashville: Abingdon Press, revised edition 2001] is one such resource.) A third is a questionnaire about lifestyle, relationships, and other information that will help me prepare for the counseling session. (Such a questionnaire is included in *Growing Love in Christian Marriage*.) I ask the couple to return the questionnaire to me several days before the session.

When the couple comes for counseling, I explain the four purposes of the session listed above. Then I spend a little time getting acquainted and making them feel comfortable. References to some of the information on the questionnaire may help with this.

Next, we read through the ritual for the wedding together, preferably the one they have chosen to use. I do a little homiletical, but not preachy, exposition on the meaning of the statements and promises included in the service. In doing this, I hope to prepare the couple to pay attention to what they will be saying and to mean it. I believe that it is important to spend some time explaining the Christian concept of love, in contrast to the ideas of love that are popular in our culture, and helping the couple see how that kind of love can lay the foundation for a happy and lasting marriage.

Then I move to counseling the couple about any issues that need attention as they prepare for marriage. Ask: "Are there any things that you may want to talk about with regard to your preparation for marriage?" Using the questionnaire, you may ask if there are any issues with regard to such things as family relationships, role expectations, plans to have children, professions, and so forth. My experience has been that counseling usually doesn't get very far in this context. The couple is not thinking about problems, and they do not yet know what questions to ask. The best thing you can do is to make them aware of areas in which problems could arise and to form a relationship to which they would be willing to return for help.

After this, turn to the plans for the wedding ceremony. Try to get clarity about how the service will be organized so you can conduct the wedding rehearsal. When time for the rehearsal comes, I try to keep it light but without allowing anything serious to be trivialized. I always end a rehearsal with a little speech that puts things into perspective. You are welcome to borrow it.

> "We all want this wedding to be something beautiful and dignified. But we don't have to make ourselves miserable to make it that. Just remember what is happening here. These two people are going to stand up before God and everyone important to them and promise to love each other for the rest of their lives. Just remember what is happening and relax and participate in it. If we do that, the service will have all of the beauty and dignity it needs. By the way, we make no mistakes in weddings. We sometimes make in-process revisions of the ritual, but no mistakes. The wedding will be perfect."

In all that you do to prepare a couple for marriage, there should be a sense of participation in the celebration of something that is truly joyful.

Baptisms are more likely to take place within the faith community and among people who have at least some commitment to the Christian faith. But there are still some who will contact the church requesting a "christening." They may have in mind a private service that will fulfill an old tradition and that will provide an occasion for a social event celebrating the birth of a baby. I recall one couple who came for pre-baptism counseling. They were not members of the church. One grandparent was an inactive member. They made it clear that they had a private service in mind. I explained that baptism is one of the sacraments of the church and that it is our tradition to celebrate it within a service of worship of the church. The man responded that he had no use at all for the church and that he had no intention of setting foot inside of one. I asked how he intended to carry out the promise he would have to make in the service of baptism to "nurture [this child] in Christ's holy church, that by your teaching and example [he or she] may be guided to accept God's grace for [him/herself], to profess [his/her] faith openly, and to lead a Christian life" (*United Methodist Hymnal*, 1989). The father apparently hadn't realized that any commitment would be part of what was expected. He went away angry. I do not know whether or not the child received baptism. But, if she did not, the baptism she did not receive would have been simply a matter of going through meaningless motions.

Baptism can make a big difference in the life of a child and of a family if the family members are serious about accepting God's gift of love and responding with commitment. But it doesn't work by magic. People who come requesting baptism for their children must be helped to understand that.

Ordinarily, the pre-baptism counseling session is a very happy occasion. In fact, the baptism of the first child is often the occasion on which a couple who have been inactive in the church will decide to act on all of their good intentions and get back into the church and let the Christian faith begin to form their family life. Reading over the ritual for infant baptism—or, in churches that don't practice infant baptism, the service for infant dedication—can give you a chance to remind the couple what the Christian faith is all about and what it can mean to their family. Make it a happy occasion that the family will want to make a turning point in their lives.

Another rich and celebrative service can come when it is time for a young person to make his or her own commitment to Christ and his church and to be confirmed as a full member of the church. You, as pastor, will hopefully have been involved in the teaching of the confirmation class that prepares young people for this commitment. It is good for other church members to be involved with the confirmands as teachers and as mentors, but it is very important for the pastor to be deeply involved.

Confirmation class will give you one of your best chances to form really significant relationships with young people. If you should stay in one parish for a number of years, those relationships formed in confirmation classes can accumulate and grow and open some really significant opportunities for ministry with the young people as they are growing up.

I have always been personally involved in confirmation classes. I have usually planned at least twelve sessions in which I was the lead teacher. Parents have appreciated this commitment. Frequently a parent has said to me, "Pastor, we can't tell you how much we appreciate the time you have spent with our young people. We know that you have much more important things to do." I haven't yet figured out what a pastor might have to do that is more important than explaining the Christian faith to young people and helping them to get ready to make a meaningful commitment of their lives to Christ and the church.

Even though the decision to be confirmed must be that of the young person himself or herself, it is important for the family to be involved in a supportive way and to celebrate the decision when it has been made. It has been my custom to end the confirmation class experience by making a call on each young person in his or her home with the parents present. There I ask the young person whether he or she is ready for confirmation. There are usually three questions: (1) Do you have any questions you want to discuss about any of what we have been over in confirmation class? (2) Do you think you understand what it means to be a Christian and a member of the church? (3) Are you ready to make your commitment and to be confirmed? As you might expect, those questions are more likely to evoke mumbled, monosyllabic answers than to bring on lengthy theological conversations. But the conversation is very meaningful. The visit can be ended with a very meaningful time of prayer. Pray for the young person, for the family, and for the church. I believe that these experiences have been very significant for the young people and the families involved. I know they have been for me.

Many functions of ministry involve pastoral care and pastoral relationships. Inviting people to serve in positions of responsibility in the church is an example. Visioning and planning meetings can become occasions for significant interactions. So can many other events in the church. I want to focus on one other aspect of the church's work that can have a significant but often overlooked relationship to pastoral care. That is evangelism.

I will not say much about evangelism because another book in this series will be dedicated to that subject. I do, however, want to point out that there is a much closer relationship between evangelism and pastoral care than many people think, especially in small membership churches. The most caring thing that anyone can do for another is to share the Christian faith with him or her. Such sharing can lead a person into a life-shaping relationship with God that can move that person toward real wholeness. As you and your church members move out into caring relationships with other people in the community, you will come into contact with people who need for someone to share the Christian faith with them. Do not miss any opportunity to share it.

Some people seem to think that evangelism requires a different kind of relationship than pastoral care, one that is more akin to salesmanship with an emphasis on closing the sale. I don't believe that is true. If a person shares a witness within the context of a caring and respectful relationship, it is much more likely to be received with appreciation. The invitation that is most likely to be accepted is one that comes from a trusted friend. The caring relationship gives credibility to a witness to the love of God. If your church becomes a welcoming fellowship of caring people, then an invitation into such a fellowship is more likely to be accepted. The relationships can enable a person who needs it an opportunity to experience the love of God instead of just hearing about it.

When you sense that someone may need to hear a witness or to receive an invitation, offer your witness simply and personally. Then wait to see what the response will be. If there seems to be some receptiveness, go further. When you sense that you have reached the limit of a person's willingness to talk about the faith, don't push any further. Wait for the person's readiness. You have time to love a person into relationship with God. That is a strategy for evangelism that can work well in a small membership church, and it is very closely related to the caring ministries of the church.

11

Pastoral Counseling

Many ministers really want to be counselors. They have a vocation for that ministry and they get satisfaction out of it. I never felt that way about it. Yet, when I was serving small membership churches in rural areas, I knew that many people in my church and community needed counseling of one kind or another. I also knew that, having had seminary training, I and a few other pastors like me were the nearest things to competent counselors that could be found in an area of several counties. If there were competent professional counselors available, many of the people who needed them felt that they could not afford them. The church needs for pastors to be ready to do pastoral counseling.

As we have said, a great deal of pastoral counseling takes place informally through the everyday conversations between a pastor and the people of the community. But sometimes a person or a family may have a problem for which a different kind of help is needed. Someone may contact you and ask for counseling. Statistical studies indicate that more people are likely to contact their pastors for counseling than any other kind of helping professional.

Thus there is a great opportunity to help. But there can be a problem in that the pastoral relationship and the counseling relationship are two different kinds of relationships. It will be necessary to work with the person who asks for counseling to move from the one relationship into the other and back again. (Richard Dayringer has a lot to say about this in part 3 of *The Heart of Pastoral Counseling.*)

Some pastors prefer to refer as many people as possible to professional counselors. Some church members have actually called me and asked for a referral rather than for counseling. There are several reasons that some pastors prefer to refer. A pastor who has not had specialized training in counseling may not feel competent to deal with the church member's problems. The pastor may not have time to adequately meet the needs of the person seeking help. The pastoral relationship may lend itself to being abused by very dependent people who will ask for more of the pastor's time and energy than she or he can afford to give. And, if the counseling relationship results in the church member needing to confess certain embarrassing things, or if it becomes necessary for the counselor to behave in certain confrontational ways, the things that take place in counseling may make it difficult for the church member to have a comfortable relationship with the pastor and the church after the counseling has been done.

In order to effectively make referrals, you will need to be acquainted with counselors and other helping agencies in your community to whom you can confidently refer people in need. It is wise to seek out these resource people and get acquainted with them as soon as possible after beginning a ministry in a new community. Insist on people who have professional training and certification. This usually will include training at the university level, some practice under supervision, and licensing either by the state or by some recognized professional organization like the American Association of Pastoral Counselors or the American Association of Marriage and Family Therapists. There are many people who advertise themselves to be counselors, especially in the religious field, who really are not trained and competent. Avoid them. Competent counselors will be glad to tell you about their qualifications. It will also be important to refer people to counselors who will have an understanding of and appreciation for the religious faith of those you refer. It will not be necessary to always insist on a counselor who professes the same religious faith that you and your church members share, but he or she must certainly be willing to work within the framework of your religious orientation. You can learn this as you get acquainted with the professionals to whom you may make referrals.

You will certainly have to deal with some people who are having problems with alcohol. There are so many of them that you can't miss it. The best thing that you can do is to put these people in touch with Alcoholics Anonymous. They have the best record in helping people with that problem. The person who needs help will have to make the call and ask for it. You can encourage her or him to do that. The telephone number will be in your directory. People with drug addiction problems will also need referral to some professional helping agency.

Once you have made a referral, stay in touch. Play a supporting role. But let the person to whom you have referred carry the ball in counseling.

However, having said all that, it may still be necessary for you to do some formal counseling. You may not feel a need to refer a person who needs counseling. You may feel capable of working with the person. And many people whom you might want to refer may not want to be referred. Some people who have built up a rapport with you may be reluctant to start over building a relationship with a stranger. Also, many may want the consciously religious perspective that counseling with a pastor can give. When it seems wise, go ahead and enter into the counseling relationship. You can always reserve the option of recommending a referral or of seeking a consultation if you find that you are in beyond your depth.

When you move from a pastoral relationship into a counseling relationship, it is best to do it in a way that makes it clear to both you and the counselee that a change is taking place. When a church member calls and asks to come in for counseling or "to talk about a problem," that understanding is already implied. When a church member brings up a problem that suggests a need for counseling in casual conversation, especially if that happens more than once, you may say, "It sounds like you may need some help with that. Would you like for me to arrange for you to see a counselor, or would you like for us to meet for some counseling sessions?"

When counseling is requested, spend the first part of the first session coming to an understanding of the "contract" that is being made between you. Have it understood that you are moving out of a regular pastoral relationship into a counseling relationship and that, when the process is over, you will move back again. Ask the counselee to define the problem with which help is needed. That will be your starting place. (But be ready to discover that the first problem mentioned may not be the real problem.) Establish a plan for meeting at a certain place for a clearly defined period of time and for a number of sessions that have been at least tentatively predetermined. If a counselee knows that he or she will be meeting with you for six one-hour sessions, he or she will be more likely to make good use of the time to move toward a solution of the problem. The counselee needs to know that everything shared in the counseling session will be kept in confidence. However, if it seems necessary, you may want to make it clear that, if the counselee confesses some criminal activity or if it becomes apparent to you that some harm may be done, either to the counselee or to someone else, you may not be able to keep that confidential. If you are working with a married couple or with a family, or with two or more people involved in a conflict, you may want to schedule some time to see each person individually as well as to see them all together. It can be especially important to agree upon a schedule in cases like that because it assures all parties of the good intentions of the others.

Finding an appropriate place for a counseling session can be a problem in small churches where there is no pastor's study with a secretary sitting outside the door. This can be especially problematic when you are working with a person of the opposite sex. You will want a place where there is privacy, where the coming and going of the counselee will not be too conspicuous, but where you will not be entirely alone. Sometimes the living room of your house will do so long as your spouse is watching television in the back bedroom. Sometimes a larger church nearby can lend you an appropriate space.

What you do in your counseling sessions will depend on the needs of the counselee. Read again the things I said earlier about the art of pastoral conversation. Those suggestions were drawn from the techniques of pastoral counseling. Many approaches to pastoral counseling have been suggested by practitioners who have studied and written in the field. Howard Clinebell has given a comprehensive survey of those approaches in the book I have recommended for further study. Most writers today suggest an eclectic approach. That means that you should learn all you can about all the different approaches to counseling and then use the approach that seems most appropriate in each situation.

It is appropriate for you to bring the resources of the Christian faith into whatever situation you and your counselee may be working through. But it is best not to do that too early in the counseling session. First, do a lot of listening. Try hard to thoroughly understand what the counselee is trying to tell you. After you have begun to understand what is going on in the life of the person with whom you are working and how he or she is feeling about it, it can be helpful to share reflection on some passage of scripture or some Christian belief that could help the person see her or his situation in the light of the Christian faith. Try to help your counselee discover the helpful resources that the Christian faith can offer. At the end of a counseling session, and sometimes at critical points during the session, it may be helpful to offer a prayer. Start by lifting the situation, as you have come to understand it, up to God. Then talk it over with God and ask for God's guidance and help. By doing this, you bring God into the conversation as an active participant.

One way to get help with your counseling and develop your counseling skills is to ask your counselee for permission to have a consultation with another professional who will not know the counselee's identity. The first step in doing that is to write a verbatim of your counseling session as soon as possible after the session has occurred. Try to remember and write down what each of you said, word for word, in each interchange of the counseling session. Make notes of any nonverbal communication that took place. If you have been as attentive as you should have been during the session, you will find that you will be more able to recall and record the exact conversation than you think. Just the process of writing the verbatim will be a sort of self-supervision. You will notice when you missed a cue or when you might have taken a different approach that could have been helpful. If, during your reflections, you notice something that you should have asked about or talked about, you can bring it up in the next session. Ask another pastor who has had some training in pastoral counseling to read over the verbatim with you and to reflect with you on what was happening in the session and how you might have given your best help. In some places, there are certified supervising counselors who can give really expert guidance for a fee. Getting a consultation can be especially helpful when you are afraid that you may be getting in beyond your depth.

It is important to watch for any signs that a referral to a person with more advanced skills may be needed. You may need to make a referral if you have reached the end of your agreed upon number of sessions and you are not close to a solution for the problem. If there is evidence that your counselee has suffered physical, sexual, or emotional abuse, you will need to encourage the counselee to either change the abusive situation or to get out of it. This can get complicated and sometimes dangerous. Consult the helping agencies in your area that work with abused people.

If you see signs of serious mental illness, you will want to talk with family members or others who could get the person the professional help he or she needs. In the book I have recommended, Howard Clinebell lists the following signs of serious mental disturbance:

> (a) Persons believe (without any basis in reality) that others are attempting to harm them, assault them sexually, or influence them in strange ways. (b) They have delusions of grandeur about themselves. (c) They show abrupt changes in their typical patterns of behavior. (d) They hallucinate, hearing nonexistent sounds or voices, or seeing nonexistent persons or things. (e) They have rigid, bizarre ideas and fears, which cannot be influenced by logic. (f) They engage in

...repetitious patterns of compulsive actions or obsessive thoughts. (g) They are disoriented (unaware of time, place, or personal identity). (h) They are depressed to the point of near-stupor or are strangely elated and/or aggressive. (i) They withdraw into their inner world, losing interest in normal activities. (Clinebell, *Basic Types of Pastoral Care & Counseling*, pp. 312-13; adapted from Clinebell, *The Mental Health Ministry of the Local Church* [Nashville: Abindgon Press, 1972], p. 244)

These conditions call for the attention of a psychiatrist.

Sometimes a person will tell you about a problem that another person is having and ask you to go and counsel with that person. This may be a person who is in conflict with a friend or a family member and he or she may want you to "fix" the other person. But sometimes it will be a caring person expressing genuine loving concern. In those cases, you will have to explain that you can only help those who come to you asking for help. You can counsel those who have come concerning *their* participation in the difficult relationship. And you can make yourself available to the person about whom they are concerned. But there is little that you can do to help someone who has not come asking for help and willing to participate with the counselor in the helping process.

I hope you understand how inadequate this treatment of the subject of pastoral counseling has been. Keep on learning.

For further study

Clinebell, Howard. *Basic Types of Pastoral Care & Counseling.* Nashville: Abingdon, 1984.

12

Helping with a Crisis

When you hear that a crisis has occurred in the life of someone in your parish, go by for a visit to express your caring concern. At first, your message may simply be, "I have heard what is going on in your life [mention what specifically you are talking about], and I want you to know that I will be thinking of you and praying for you. If there is anything else I can do for you, please call on me." Then it is important to listen carefully to the response that the person makes. If the person is coping well with the crisis, that simple expression of pastoral concern may be all that is needed. But if the person is not coping well, and asks you to help, you may be called on for a kind of pastoral care called "crisis intervention." In fact, you may sometimes receive a call from some emotionally distraught church member who wants to tell you about something bad that has happened to him or her and who specifically asks you to come and talk about it. That may happen with some frequency after you have become well acquainted. I had only been in my first parish a few weeks when one of the older ladies in the church sent word that she needed my help. She had received a message that her alcoholic son-in-law had committed suicide and she didn't know what to do. In fact, the message was not true; the son-in-law was staging a manipulative farce. But it involved me immediately in a complex situation with people who needed help resolving a crisis.

Usually, the crisis is brought on by some happening: a job has been lost, a child has gotten into trouble, a spouse has asked for a divorce, there has been a business failure, a home was destroyed by fire, a loved one was killed in a traffic accident. Happenings like that are big enough to upset anyone. But, quite often, the event that triggers the crisis may be something much smaller, something the person should have been able to take in stride; but because of complicating factors or emotional conditions, the person isn't able to cope. The person involved may perceive the situation as a threat. Anxiety may build up in ways that get in the way of coping. Then a person may need help in getting things under control. You, as pastor, may be called on to offer that help.

David Switzer, who has written extensively about the pastor's role in crisis intervention, suggests the following steps.

You should start by offering help. If the offer is accepted, move into a helping relationship. Let the person tell you what has happened and what she or he is experiencing. It may actually be necessary for you to help the person identify what it is that has them so upset. Let the person express his or her feelings, including any feelings of fear, guilt, or anger. Be understanding and accepting of all that is shared with you. Then begin to build up hope by helping the person believe that he or she will be able to find a way through the crisis.

When the person seems ready to go on to the next step, help him or her get the situation into focus. Talk to the person about all aspects of the situation. Help the person identify what seems threatening and what is the source of the anxiety.

Then move on to help the person learn to cope. Help him or her identify the resources that are available for solving the problem. Make a list of possibilities. Help the person think through the decisions that must be made and choose the actions that must be taken. Help the person get in touch with other people who can be of assistance. Sometimes you can mobilize the resources of the parish to help with specific problems. Finally, help the person reflect on the experience and assimilate any learning that may have taken place.

All these steps may take several weeks of rather intensive pastoral involvement. It may be necessary for you to be in touch with the person several times a week to give emotional support and to help the person think through courses of action. It is your role, not to take the problem out of the hands of the person who owns it, but to help that person cope creatively.

There is one kind of request for crisis help that may need a little more reflection. A person may come to the pastor for help in some kind of a financial crisis asking you for help in finding money to meet an emergency need. This may be a legitimate need to which you and the parish will want to respond. But in some cases it may be an abuse of the parish's caring function. You will eventually meet the indigent transient who has his or her story so well organized and rehearsed that you will know you are hearing an oft-repeated recitation. One of the biggest challenges in caring ministries is learning how best to respond to that kind of request. Churches, or better yet, groups of churches, must find ways of responding to real needs without being exploited by those who are chronically in crisis. They may provide funds for emergency assistance and also counseling in financial management. Dealing with this kind of request is different from real crisis intervention. It is useful to recognize the difference and find appropriate ways to deal with it.

For further study

Switzer, David K. *Pastoral Care Emergencies*. Minneapolis: Fortress Press, 2000, chapter 3.
———. *The Minister as Crisis Counselor*. Nashville: Abingdon, 1986.

13

Dealing with Conflict in the Church

Everyone wants harmony in the church. You, as pastor, probably want it more than anyone else. But conflict happens, and it sometimes—not always, but sometimes—turns hurtful. It is your job as pastor to try to keep conflicts creative, to resolve as many conflicts as you can, and to try to facilitate the healing of any hurts that result from the conflicts—even when you are one of the parties in the conflict.

Conflict management in churches is actually a very complex and difficult aspect of the ministry. A complete study of conflict management probably belongs in the area of pastoral leadership or administration. In this context, I will share a few thoughts about the dimensions of the subject that relate to pastoral care. For a more complete treatment, see the book I have recommended for further study.

Conflict over significant issues ought to be expected. Creative thinking and decisive action naturally generate conflict. In small membership churches, change—even important, obviously necessary change—will probably cause conflict. So does prophetic preaching on the big issues of the day. But friends can disagree over issues and still be friends. You will be much more effective in giving leadership and in forming Christian convictions if you keep the conversation going on in the context of relationships of mutual respect and appreciation. That should be one of your primary objectives as pastor-leader.

Unfortunately, some conflicts become hurtful. The most hurtful conflicts are those that are, in reality, petty little conflicts between people who don't like each other or who are competing for status or control. Some pastors find themselves in churches where there are divisions that have been crippling the church for generations. Some divisions and conflicts may have been going on for so long that everyone has forgotten what they were all about in the first place. If you find yourself in one of those situations, try to avoid being drawn into the conflict. Avoid being identified with, or being claimed by, one party or the other. Try hard to build relationships with people in all of the groups in the church. Try to have a ministry of reconciliation. Try to find some mission on which all the people can work together. Pray for a miracle.

Even in the life of a healthy church, there will be conflicts. Sometimes people will be hurt by them. You should do what you can to heal those hurts.

A number of years ago, a minister by the name of John S. Savage noticed that, in old photographs of church activities, he saw pictures of people who had once been active members of the church but whom he had never met. At first he thought they might have been people who had moved away. But when he asked about them, he learned that they were still living in the community but had been alienated from the church in one way or another. He did a research project on what had happened to those people and how such losses might be avoided. He published his findings in a book entitled *The Apathetic and Bored Church Member: Psychological and Theological Implications* (Pitsford, NY: Lead Consultants, 1976; now out of print). Here are some of the things we can learn from that book.

Many times, when people have experienced a hurt or disappointment in the church or come into conflict with someone in the church, they will send a message that they are unhappy by being absent. It is important for you and church leadership to notice when people have been absent and find out why. That should not be hard to do in a small membership church. If the church member is sending a message through the absence, the church and you should recognize that and respond as quickly as possible. Not to respond is to send the message, "We didn't miss you and, if there is something wrong, we don't care." That is not the message you want to send. In fact, some people will send a message about their unhappiness much more directly, usually by complaining to someone who they know will report their griev-ance to you. When such a message has been received, the church has only a limited amount of time to respond. If the response does not come, the unhappy person is likely to become a dropout or to go to another church. The sooner the response is made, the bet-ter the chance of repairing the relationship.

When you get the message that a church member is unhappy, someone needs to respond by making a visit to the unhappy per-son. Unless there is a good friend of the person or a trained lay visitor who could do it better, that person is likely to be you. I don't know anyone who enjoys making this kind of visit. But it needs to be done. The sooner you do it, the better.

Call and ask for an appointment. It is best not to just drop by. Explain the reason for your visit. "I have heard that there has been some unhappiness, and I would like to come by and talk with you about it." The person will probably be willing for you to come. If the person seems unwilling for you to come, try to pro-long the telephone conversation to accomplish as much as possi-ble of the agenda that we will outline for the visit. A face-to-face visit is much better.

When you visit, start by assuring the person that he or she is important to the church and that you care how he or she is feel-ing. Then invite the person to tell you what has happened to cause the bad feelings. Let the feelings be expressed. It is impor-tant for you to listen to what the unhappy church member has to say and to appreciate her or his feelings. Reflective responses help the person know he or she has been heard: "I hear you saying that you had some really strong feelings about the issue that was before the board last month and that you didn't agree with the decision that was made." If the person says, "That's right," then you have let him or her know that the message has been received. If you don't get that response, keep on listening and reflecting until you do.

If, in fact, the person has called to your attention something that is really wrong, you might try to think of ways to fix it. If there is a conflict with another church member, you might act as mediator to try to resolve it. Quite often, you will just have to try to do "damage control" after some unhappy thing has happened.

If the person is expressing a strong opinion or disagreement with something the church is doing, listen to it. Urge the person to express those opinions in the proper decision-making settings if it is not too late for that. If strong feelings of hurt or anger are expressed, just receive them and reflect, "I understand that you are really angry about this." Remember that, unless the bad feelings really are directed at you, you do not need to absorb them, just accept them. It is best not to argue with the person's opinions or feelings or to try to defend the church or the offending person. Just say something like, "I am really sorry that you had that bad experience. We want you to know that you are important to us. We hope you will come back to the church and give things a chance to work out."

You will then have to wait to see where the unhappy church member goes from there. That one visit may be all that is needed to renew the relationship. I have seen that happen several times. Once I made a get-acquainted call on an inactive member and found that she was not coming to church because she had been in the hospital and I had not visited her. It had happened soon after I came to the church. I did not know everyone. Someone had told me about her illness, but I had misunderstood and visited the wrong person. When I finally got to see her, she told me about her displeasure. I apologized. That was all that was necessary. She started attending church again. But in many cases, further work of reconciliation may be needed.

The unhappy church member may never be able to find his or her way back into the fellowship of the church. But, as pastor, you should do all you can do to give things a chance to work out happily. Of course, some people are tenuously related to the church and change churches frequently. And some may be using their absence and the threat of leaving the church as a power play to gain control. One pastor observed that it had been important for him to learn not to "beat himself up" every time someone dropped out. But as the pastor, you must do all you can to keep the sheep together in the flock. If you do not do your part, you are very likely to regret it.

Of course, the most painful conflicts are those in which you yourself are in conflict with some person or group within the church or the community. If you are dealing with the kind of conflict that happens normally when things are happening in a healthy church, do your best to keep the conflicts constructive. Be careful to keep the conflict focused on the issues. Don't let it degenerate into critical attacks on personalities. Go to some extra trouble to maintain a good personal relationship with those with whom you are in conflict. Friends can disagree over issues and still be friends. Unless some matter of Christian belief or of the integrity of the church and its mission is involved, be ready to lose a battle in order to win the war. Things that really need to be done will probably be done eventually. Or, it is just possible that you may discover that some issue was not as important as you thought it was.

Sometimes, in spite of your best efforts, you will find yourself not having a good relationship with some church members. You are human. So are they. Sometimes, you make mistakes. Sometimes personalities just don't mesh. Nobody can be everybody's favorite pastor. When you find yourself in unhappy or conflictual relationships, be ready to do all you can to repair the relationship. If you can't build a better relationship, then you must find ways of working with the people with whom you do not have a good relationship, and with all the other members of the church, to accomplish the greater purpose to which you are all committed.

The first thing you have to do is get your ego into perspective. Remember that what is going on in the church is not primarily about you. It is about the purpose of God for the creation. It is about the loving work of God in the world through Jesus Christ.

It is about the God-given mission of the church. We must be able to say, "It's OK with me if you liked the last pastor better than you like me so long as we can work together now to do the work of the Lord." Putting your own ego in its proper place can open the way to the resolution of many conflicts.

If you have made a mistake or been insensitive or hurt some person's feelings, go to that person and apologize. Do what you can to rebuild the relationship. If someone has done something hurtful to you, forgive. To forgive is to set an offense aside so that it does not restrict or destroy a relationship. Forgiving is an important concept for Christians. It describes a part of what God does for us and a part of what God expects us to do for others. If we will practice what we preach, that will do a lot to build loving relationships within a church family.

Unfortunately, sometimes even your best efforts will not be able to heal hurtful relationships. Some people may lack the inner wholeness they need to forgive your mistakes. Some emotionally unhealthy people may just not like you for reasons that even they cannot fully understand. And there may be some who have certain theological or political or social action (or inaction) agendas that they hope to push by attacking you. Sometimes it is helpful to bring in someone, possibly a denominational official, to act as mediator to resolve conflicts. Every pastor I know, certainly including myself, carries some hurting injuries suffered in conflicts that just couldn't be resolved. We need healing too.

If things get really bad, give special attention to maintaining your own physical, mental, and spiritual health. Seek out support groups among the clergy or laity who will affirm your personhood. If you can see that the hostility directed at you really should be directed elsewhere, don't absorb it. Recognize that you are dealing with people who have problems and try to make compassionate pastoral responses to their needs. You will be surprised how that one attitude can change the complexion of many conflicted situations. If the conflict is over an issue, ask yourself if it is a really important issue. If the issue is important for the church or for the kingdom of God, stand your ground. Try to win others over by loving action. If you can't work things out, remember that there are other churches. Sometimes it is best to move on and let some other pastor have a chance to do what needs to be done. You can make a fresh start in another place.

For further study

Lott, David B., editor. *Conflict Management in Congregations*. Bethesda, MD: The Alban Institute, 2001.

14

Maintaining Integrity

Much of the church's ability to minister depends upon its ability to win and keep the confidence of the people with whom it works. That is especially true in this postmodern age in which people do not trust institutions and theological systems as they once did. It is important for the church as a whole to behave in a trustworthy way and for ministers of the church to live up to the highest standards of personal and relational integrity.

People need to believe that the church cares about them and that it is motivated in all that it does by a desire to do something good for them rather than by any desire to exploit them or use them for the purposes of the institution. This should be in the mind of every church planning committee, every Sunday school teacher, every evangelistic visitor, and every care team member as they go about doing their work. It must certainly be in your mind as you go about the work of pastoring. It is not enough just to appear to be a caring person. It is essential to actually be a caring person. In small membership churches, people will know the difference. This must be a matter of spiritual growth, not just of cultivating an appearance. It is important for the pastor to be real.

One very important expression of relational integrity is the ability to maintain the confidentiality of pastoral conversations. A person must be able to believe that anything shared with a pastor in a counseling session or other pastoral conversation will be kept confidential. I have mentioned some exceptions to this rule that apply to criminal activity, abuse, and threats to the well-being of the counselee or others.

It is wise to develop the habit of not talking about what is going on in the lives of others, even when the information did not come in confidential conversation. Gossip is hurtful. It is important for the pastor and other church members not to get a reputation for participating in it.

Sometimes someone will share something with you in a counseling situation that you would like to use as an illustration in a sermon. Be very careful about doing that. Choose only those stories that present the person involved in a good light. Ask permission to share the story. And when you share it, explain that you have permission to share it. Resist the temptation to tell the congregation about the problems you know about in the lives of church members, even when they illustrate needs that you know are shared by many people. When preparing sermons that apply the resources of the Christian faith to the needs that you know exist in your congregation, be careful not to make anyone feel singled out and talked about in the sermon. If people hear you talking in church about things that you have learned in counseling sessions, they will be very reluctant to share with you anything that they don't want known by everybody.

Another concern having to do with integrity is the whole area of sexual misconduct. If you have been reading the newspapers, you know how important that is. The moral failures of high profile church leaders make headlines and do tremendous damage to the reputation of the church. When these failures occur in the life of a small membership church, the circle of devastation may be smaller, but the damage will be deeper and last longer. The news about the mistakes some churches have made in covering up sexual misconduct instead of confronting it has undermined the confidence that many people once had in the church.

In an effort to repair the damage done by these failures, a rather stringent set of guidelines is emerging. According to these guidelines, no adult minister, leader, teacher, or youth counselor should ever be left alone with a group of children or young people and certainly never with a single child or young person. No minister should ever be socially involved with (that is, date) any counselee or church member or any other person who could be perceived to be in a subordinate position to the minister. No uninvited physical contact or conversation that could be considered suggestive should ever take place between a minister and another person. You have noticed that I have frequently mentioned the importance of not being alone with a member of the opposite sex.

Frankly, these rules are awfully hard to live by. They are especially hard on young single ministers serving small community churches. You may not always be able to avoid being alone with a person of the opposite sex, but you should try. If you must make visits to persons of the opposite sex, if possible make them during daylight hours, take along your spouse or another church member, and avoid making repetitive visits. Be very careful not to make any uninvited physical contact. Hugs may be needed. But be very careful about when, where, and how you give them.

The atmosphere is so charged with suspicion these days that you must sometimes go to extremes to avoid any appearance of misconduct. One day I was in a public swimming pool playing with my two young grandsons. We were having a great time. They were climbing all over me. I was throwing them up in the air and letting them splash back into the water. Eventually, a little girl who was in the pool came over and wanted to play too. My wife, who was sitting beside the pool, called to me and said, "It's time to go." I got out of the pool and asked why we had to go so early. She said, "You don't know that little girl or her family. If someone accused you of touching her inappropriately, your whole career in the ministry could go down the drain." She was right. It is sad that we live in that kind of a world—but we do.

These cautions are troublesome but important. They are meant not just to avoid any appearance of impropriety, but also to help you keep any unfortunate relationships from actually developing. Both you and your church members are sexual beings and capable of being tempted. Temptation can develop before you know it.

Do you think it could never happen to you? Imagine this scenario. Sally is an attractive woman whose life has been hard and not at all like the glamorous lives of the people she sees every day on the soap operas. A secret discontent has been growing inside of her for a long time. Sally is married to John. John is a good man who loves his family and works hard to support them. But John works as a mechanic in a garage and comes home dirty every day. Besides that, John drinks beer, cusses, and doesn't know how to make his wife feel good about herself. Part of Sally's discontent focuses on John. Sally begins to think about the pastor. He is always clean and well dressed and well spoken. He is a caring person and knows how to be thoughtful of another person's needs. Sally begins to fantasize about what it would be like to be with him instead of with John. Eventually, she may communicate her feelings, either intentionally or unintentionally, to the pastor. If that should happen at a time when the pastor is going through a time of discontent of his own, perhaps a time when his own wife, who knows the truth about his humanity, has not been too responsive, then the stage is set for something to happen that could be awkward, embarrassing, or tragic. (You can imagine a similar scenario involving a clergywoman.) The best course is to avoid allowing situations to develop that could be troublesome.

One thing that pastors can do to keep themselves out of harm's way is to pay attention to their own physical, mental, and spiritual health. A psychologist was coaching a group of pastors, of which I was a member, on their counseling skills. One day he asked, "What should you do when you find yourself having inappropriate feelings for a counselee of the opposite sex?" We suggested all sorts of solutions. Most of them had to do with white-knuckled determination to do what is right. The psychologist said, "When I find that happening to me, I check up on myself. I usually find that I have been working too hard and not having enough fun. I plan some time off and take my wife out for a nice evening." The psychologist had taught the ministers what it means to be saved through grace.

By all means, keep yourself spiritually healthy so that temptations will not occur. But when they do occur (not *if* but *when*), if grace doesn't save you, remember that the law is also a gift from God who loves us. Remember that the "Thou shalt not!" has a role to play. The gospel of which you are called to be a servant is the hope of the world. It is much too important for us to allow it to be discredited in the eyes of the world because some clergyperson was irresponsible.

15

Providing for the Needs of the Pastor and the Pastor's Family

The church, the world, and God expect a lot from ministers. They need for ministers to be basically healthy people, secure in their personhood and able to be honest about themselves, spiritually alive and attractive, and able to reach out to others in genuine and effective loving care. Most ministers who take their work seriously find themselves working sixty hours a week more often than the traditional forty. Churches are expecting more and more from their ministers and understanding less. Many more pastors are fired by their churches than should be. The ministry can sometimes be a lonely and thankless job. For that reason, ministers must be very intentional about establishing boundaries and making provision for their own physical, emotional, and spiritual health and that of their families.

It is important to keep these circumstances in perspective. If you ever come to think of the church as your enemy, you will be undone. Things will all go downhill from there. But then, neither should the pastor think of the job as a god who demands complete and sacrificial commitment. God is God. God cares about the church and about the rest of the world and about your family—and about you. God wants you to care about all those things

93

too. Make your primary commitment to God, and God will help you keep your other commitments in balance.

I remember something I did right after I had my first assignment to a church that had some potential for growth. I made a study of what I was doing with every minute of my week in the hope that I could find ways of putting more hours of effort into my work. I was working many eighty-hour weeks. I thought that if I could just put more time into my work, I could be a more successful pastor. I was "very dedicated." In retrospect, I know that I was dedicated to my own career rather than to the kingdom of God. There is a difference between those two. I needed to discover that. You may need to discover it too. A number of years later, I found myself going through the same motions of analyzing my use of time, but I was doing it for another reason. I was trying to see how I could get my work done in sixty hours a week or fewer so there would be time for myself and for my family.

After you have been in the ministry and in your parish and have had an opportunity to assess the needs, plan your workweek with "time on" and "time off." Some time shortly after the get-acquainted calls have been completed would be a good time to plan the schedule. Plan a tentative schedule that will allow you time to get done the things that need to be done. Plan a time for going to work in the morning. It can be easy for pastors, especially beginning pastors in small churches, to drop into overly permissive schedules and not to work very hard. If that happens, you can be assured that the church members will notice it. It will also be easy for you to spend too much time on functions that you enjoy and too little on others. You have a job. Be responsible about planning a schedule that allows you to get your job done. Understand that your schedule will require you to work on weekends and on some evenings, since visitation and meetings must be done at times when the people with whom you work will be free to participate. But plan a schedule that allows at least one full day and several evenings a week off for you and your family. Roy Oswald, a clergy consultant who works with the Alban Institute, insists that a minister's workweek should be no more than fifty hours long and that it should provide two days off so that there will be time for study, spiritual formation, personal health, and family relationships. (See the book I have recommended for further study.)

It is a good discipline and also a wise piece of pastor-parish relations to share your schedule with the lay leaders of your church so that you can have agreement about what you are doing. Many church members really don't know what you do or how long you work. I heard one hard-working farmer complain because he saw his pastor sitting on the parsonage porch reading a book right in the middle of the workday. If a person is accustomed to doing manual labor, he may have a hard time understanding that you are working if you are not sweating and growing calluses. Help people understand what you do.

It is very important for both you and your church members to understand that you are working on a flexible schedule. The flexible schedule needs to work both ways. You will be on call to respond to emergencies. And there will be times when the church's program will encroach on what should be your time off. You should have an understanding with your church and with yourself that you should be able to take some additional time off ("comp time") to make up for that.

You will need to establish some boundaries to protect the personal aspects of your life. Much is said about the burden of being on call for emergencies twenty-four hours a day. The truth of the matter is that the real emergencies do not come so frequently that they become oppressive, even in a fairly large church. Of course you will want to respond when there is a death or a crisis in the life of any of the families of your church. One time on Christmas Day, it was difficult to balance priorities when I received a call telling me that one of the saints had died just as my children were opening their packages. It was difficult, but we did it. And when a member family asks you to hold a funeral on what was scheduled to be your day off, you will want to modify your schedule. You will want to respond if you can to such significant occurrences. But there are always some who perceive their needs to be greater and more urgent than they really are. And in an active church, there are always a million little busy things to be done. It is these little things, not the real emergencies, that can overwhelm a pastor and his family. It is important for you to ask your church to be understanding of your need for time for yourself and your family.

You will need to plan to make good use of that time. Part of the life-shaping dynamic of the Christian faith is the balance between the *demanding* aspects of the faith and of life (the law, calling), and the *enabling* aspects (grace). It would be good for you to invite your family to share the demands of the calling and the satisfactions that go with it. It is also important to incorporate into your life and the life of your family those things that heal and build up and enable. What spiritual disciplines bring new life to your spirit? What must you do to see that the nourishment and exercise and rest necessary for physical health are provided? Where can you find stimulus for learning and growth in insight and understanding? Where do you experience fun, especially fun shared with your family? What makes life enjoyable for you and yours? See that these things are built into your life and that of your family.

Friendships are important. Cultivate some significant and lasting relationships with lay and clergy friends. Participating in share groups or support groups or covenant discipleship groups can be very valuable. Without relationships like that, the ministry can be very lonely. Look to find some mentor, some counselor, some friend to whom you can go when you need a pastor. There will be times when you will need to be ministered to.

As you get acquainted with the people of your church, some of them will become personal friends. They will be the people about your age, with families like yours, and with whom you share common interests. It is natural for friendships to develop. However, some church members may think you are showing partiality to those members with whom you spend the most time. Be very careful not to actually show partiality. Be the pastor of all the people. Then ask for understanding of your needs for friendship. Sometimes there will be conflicts between the requirements of your work and the needs of your family. Of course you will sometimes have to work when you would rather be spending time with your children. That just goes with having a job. When you have planned a schedule that allows you to get your work done and to respond to the needs of the people in your church and community and that also provides time for yourself and for your family, do your best to maintain the boundaries between these claims on your time. Sometimes there will be conflicts between the demands of your work and the needs of your family that will require you to work out some priorities. An important meeting is scheduled when you had planned an anniversary celebration with your spouse. Someone calls and asks for crisis counseling during your child's birthday party. A funeral is needed the day after you were scheduled to leave on a family vacation. When these conflicts occur, try to come up with a creative solution that will allow you to do both. Sometimes you can. If you can't, you will have to set some priorities. It is best not to set standing priorities in which the needs of the family always come first, the needs of the church always come second, and your personal needs come third, or vise versa so that one can always trump the others. All of these are high priority commitments. Instead, ask yourself, *In which of these places am I needed most right now?* Sometimes very important functions can be carried on without your presence. Sometimes another person—a lay leader or caring team member or another pastor—can stand in for you. If you have to ask to be excused from giving some requested service, call the person most directly involved and explain why. Offer to arrange for someone else to help. Make an appointment to come around for a visit later. More often than not, conflicts can be worked out without much damage.

In most situations, church members will understand your need for family time and personal time. So long as there is a plan that will allow you to meet the congregation's needs as well as your own, church members will usually be glad to help you work according to your plan and to respect your boundaries.

For further study

Oswald, Roy M. *Clergy Self-Care*. Bethesda, MD: Alban Institute, 1991.

16

Involving Laypeople in Pastoral Care

So far, this book has focused primarily upon the role of the pastor in caring ministries. In a small membership church, both the pastor and the congregation might be tempted to assume that pastoral care is the role of the pastor alone. But to give in to that temptation would be to impoverish the ministry of the church. Caring ministries should be part of the ministry of the whole congregation. It should be an important part of the work of the pastor to recruit, train, and enable lay members of the church for the work of caring. This should not be understood as the pastor recruiting laypeople to help with the pastor's work. Instead, it should be seen as the pastor enabling the whole church to do its work.

Caring ministries in a congregation can be developed in several ways and to several levels. It is important to develop a network of caring relationships within the church. Small membership churches have a unique ability to become intimate fellowships in which the members all know and care for one another and in which the network of caring relationships reaches out into the community beyond the congregation. Many of the people who choose to join a small membership church do so in the hope that they will be able to be part of such a caring fellowship.

But it would be a mistake to assume that, just because a church is small, it is a warm, caring community. Some are not. Some can be quite selfish in their orientation, thinking only of serving the needs of their own people. Some can allow themselves to be dominated by a few snobbish, negative, or critical people. And even some of those churches that do have a warm, caring fellowship among their members may have unintentionally become quite exclusive because it is hard for new people to get into the tight little circle of old friends. Small membership churches must decide intentionally to become caring fellowships.

You and the church members can work together to develop a caring fellowship. You can work at helping all the members, especially the newer members, to form significant friendships within the church. Being aware of the needs of others and lifting them up in prayer during worship services can help. Organizing responses to known needs should be a part of the congregation's ministry. Taking food to families in which there has been a serious illness or a death or into which a new baby has been born is a tradition in many churches. It is a good start. Other, more complex, needs may call for a carefully planned response. Don't forget to recognize and celebrate the joys and accomplishments of church members. That too is a way of caring. If these kinds of caring ministries are not already part of the life of a congregation, a caring pastor can be the catalyst to get them started.

The pastor can also recruit and enable laypeople whose contribution to the life of the church will be as parts of a team of caregivers. This will be their ministry. You can soon recognize those church members who are naturally caring persons and who have the gifts and the calling to do this work. You will probably find that these people are already visiting the sick and the shutins and doing other kinds of caring ministry. These may be the people who know when someone is in need of pastoral care and call you to tell you about it. Still others may come forward when you offer a training course in caring ministries. Look for the people who genuinely care about the needs of others and want to help. Avoid involving the community busybodies who get self-gratification out of tending to other people's business.

There can be a definite advantage in involving the caregivers of the congregation in an organized ministry of the church. These people can be recognized as representatives of the church. They can go into a hospital room or a home and say, "I am one of the visitors from your church." Their work can be organized so that all the needs are met and no one is overlooked. These people should be asked specifically to be members of the caring team of the church. They will need some basic training in the functions of caring ministry. Selective use of some of the material in this book can be used for this purpose. The chapters "Learning the Art of Pastoral Conversation," "Visiting Shut-ins," "Ministering to the Sick," "Ministering to the Terminally Ill," and "Ministering to the Grieving" can be especially helpful for this purpose. Once trained, the care team members should be presented to the congregation and recognized as lay ministers of the church. Then the pastor will need to help the team members organize their efforts to accomplish specific tasks like visiting the hospitals on the days when the pastor is not going, visiting the shut-ins, and giving long-term support to the grieving.

Some churches go even further in organizing and enabling lay caregivers. Programs like Stephen Ministries give much more extensive training in the skills of caregiving and assign lay caregivers to work with people who have more serious problems. Stephen Ministries is a well-developed program for which congregations have to register and send lay leaders to seminars for training. (For information, write to Stephen Ministries, 2045 Innerbelt Business Center Drive, Saint Louis, Missouri 63114-5765, or call 314/428-2600.)

Some churches may want to develop programs of caring outreach as parts of their mission to the community. Many churches organize ministries to the people in the nursing homes of their communities. Earl Shelp and Ron Sunderland have developed a kind of ministry called Sustaining Presence, through which hundreds of laypeople have become involved in helping with the care of patients with Alzheimer's or AIDS, or other patients whose needs are too great for their families alone to meet. There are many other needs for caring ministries in every community. A church that gets organized to do that kind of work can truly be a church in mission.

For further study

Shelp, Earl E. and Ronald H. Sunderland. *Sustaining Presence.* Nashville: Abingdon Press, 2000.

Conclusion

The story of the Christian church began with God caring about the people of the world and sending Jesus to make a loving response to our needs. Now, Jesus has entrusted that work to the church. It is the mission of the church and its clergy to care about all those for whom God cares and to be the agent of God's loving response to human need in the world today. Many of us believe that is the most important thing going on in our world. It is the hope of the world.

I began this book with a reflection on the beginning of my ministry. Let me end with a reflection from the end of a forty-five-year ministry. I hope that when you come to the end of your ministry, you find, as many of us have found, that there is great satisfaction in having invested your life, or some significant part of it, in the most important thing that is going on in the world. Any investment in the service of that purpose has been life well spent. But you may find, as many of us have found, that the services for which you were most appreciated and which you remember with the greatest satisfaction will be not the sermons you have preached or the successful programs you have implemented or the budgets you have met or the buildings you have built, but rather the caring relationships through which you have been able to share the life-giving, life-shaping love of God. May God give you love to share and effectiveness in sharing it.